Complete B Scales & Arpeggios In Tablature For Guitar

Howard R. Wallach

Cover photo: San Dimas guitar courtesy of Jackson / Charvel Guitar Company.

Graphics by Juan Manuel Traslavina

Exclusive Distributor - JT Publication / Heartland Music Inc.
800-447-0948

D235

Table Of Contents

Introduction 5

How To Use This Book 6

Major Scales 8

Minor Scales 12

    Natural Minor 15

    Harmonic Minor 18

    Melodic Minor 21

    Jazz Melodic Minor 26

    Hungarian Minor 29

    Rumanian Minor 32

Pentatonic Scales 36

    Major Pentatonic 38

    Minor Pentatonic 41

    Minor Pentatonic Blues 44

Modes 47

    Locrian 49

    Dorian 52

    Phrygian 55

    Lydian 59

    Mixolydian 62

Symmetrical Scales_____67

   Half Step / Whole Step Diminished_____70

   Whole Step / Half Step Diminished_____72

   Whole Tone_____74

   Augmented_____76

   Chromatic_____78

Arpeggios_____79

   Major_____80

   Minor_____81

   Augmented_____82

   Diminished Seventh_____83

   Half Diminished Seventh (m7 b5)_____85

   Dominant Seventh_____86

   Dominant Seventh b5_____87

   Dominant Seventh #5_____88

   Major Seventh_____89

   Minor Seventh_____90

   Minor / Major Seventh_____91

   Major Sixth_____92

   Minor Sixth_____93

   Major Ninth_____94

   Dominant Ninth_____95

   Minor Ninth_____96

Howard Wallach was born in Cleveland, Ohio where at the age of ten he began performing on both the jazz and classical guitar. After studying with guitar virtuoso Miguel Rubio at the Conservatory of Lausanne, Switzerland, he completed his Bachelor of Music at the Peabody Conservatory of John Hopkins University under the renowned educator Aaron Shearer. His graduate studies were undertaken at the University of Houston.

Mr. Wallach has given many solo and ensemble performances on both the guitar and lute in Switzerland, Baltimore, Houston, Washington, D.C., Cleveland and Philadelphia. Currently residing in Houston, he teaches at Houston Community College and at Lee College in Baytown, Texas.

INTRODUCTION

In my experience as a performer and teacher of the guitar I have found a great need for a book which contains all scales and arpeggios used in every kind of music by the contemporary guitarist. This book does exactly that in a systematized fashion with fingerings which are both logical and muscularly efficient for the hand.

In addition, whether the guitarist reads music or not, it is necessary to memorize the scale and arpeggio patterns by forming visual images of them on the fingerboard. For this reason, I have written the book in tablature. There is, as well, an advantage for the guitarist who is used to reading standard notation insofar as it enables him to bypass the intermediate step between reading the notation and forming the visual image. The guitarist not used to reading tablature will find himself reading it easily within the first few minutes of using the book, so long as he follows the few simple instructions given on the pages labeled "How To Use This Book".

Many professional guitarists and teachers who have seen this book have said, "This is the book I wish I'd had twenty years ago". This is not a book of music theory. It is a practical manual to the complete mastery of all scales and arpeggios on the fingerboard for the contemporary guitarist.

HOW TO USE THIS BOOK
Symbols Used In This Book

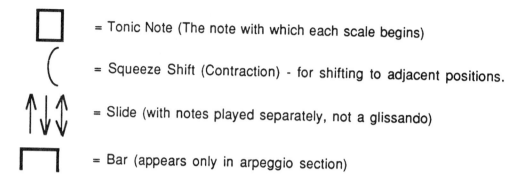

☐ = Tonic Note (The note with which each scale begins)

(= Squeeze Shift (Contraction) - for shifting to adjacent positions.

↑↓↑ = Slide (with notes played separately, not a glissando)

⊓ = Bar (appears only in arpeggio section)

Left Hand Finger Designations
0 = Open String
1 = Index
2 = Middle
3 = Ring
4 = Little

How To Read The Tablature

Always begin with the boxed note, which is the tonic of the scale. Play note by note in the ascending direction until you reach the highest sounding note indicated. From that note, then play in the descending direction until you reach the lowest sounding note indicated. If that note is not the tonic then play in the ascending direction again, until you reach the tonic. Remember, always begin and end on the boxed note.

First Position Scales
Example: G Major

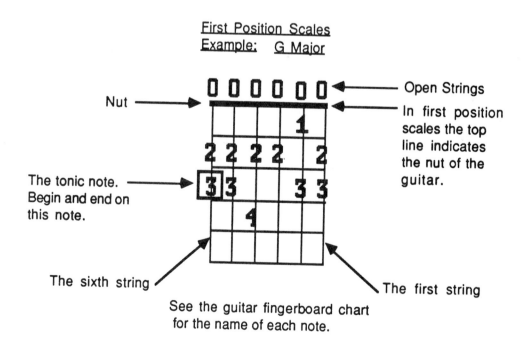

Nut →

The tonic note. Begin and end on this note. →

The sixth string

The first string

Open Strings

In first position scales the top line indicates the nut of the guitar.

See the guitar fingerboard chart for the name of each note.

6

Movable and Long Movable Scales
Example: Harmonic Minor

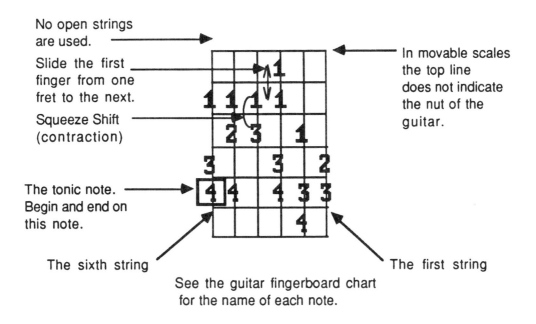

No open strings are used.

Slide the first finger from one fret to the next.

Squeeze Shift (contraction)

In movable scales the top line does not indicate the nut of the guitar.

The tonic note. Begin and end on this note.

The sixth string

The first string

See the guitar fingerboard chart for the name of each note.

Place the finger indicated within the box on the fret corresponding to the tonic of the desired scale. Use the fingerboard chart to locate the various positions of each tonic on the fourth, fifth, and sixth strings.

Each scale (except for the symmetrical scales) is presented in three ways. First, in every key in the first position, secondly in five **movable** forms and thirdly, in long movable form. While many guitarists do not play a great deal in first position, their musical ear will benefit by at least reading through the first position scales, hearing them sounded with open strings.

The five **movable** forms cover laterally on the fingerboard all practical and muscularly efficient finger patterns necessary for a complete grasp of the basic scale forms. These must be mastered before attempting the long movable scale forms, since the latter are made up of portions of the former. The long movable forms are labeled according to which of the five movable forms with which they begin. Lastly, notice that in the long movable forms, the tonic is boxed every time it appears. The symmetrical scales are given only in the first position and in the movable fashions in which they are used.

THE MAJOR SCALE

Below is the pattern of half steps and whole steps of the major scale. The straight line indicates whole steps, the "v" shaped symbol indicates the half steps.

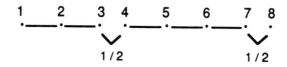

Major scales are used with (played against) the following kinds of chords:

Major (MJ)
Major 7th (MJ7)
Major sus 4 (MJ sus 4)
Major 6th (MJ6)
Major 9th (MJ9)
Major 6/9 (MJ 6/9)

Remember, all the LONG movable major scale patterns, with a couple of exceptions, begin with the second finger. The exceptions are: the E Major Scale that begins with the open sixth string (the lowest note) and the F Major Scale that begins with the first finger on the first fret of the sixth string.

First Position Major Scales

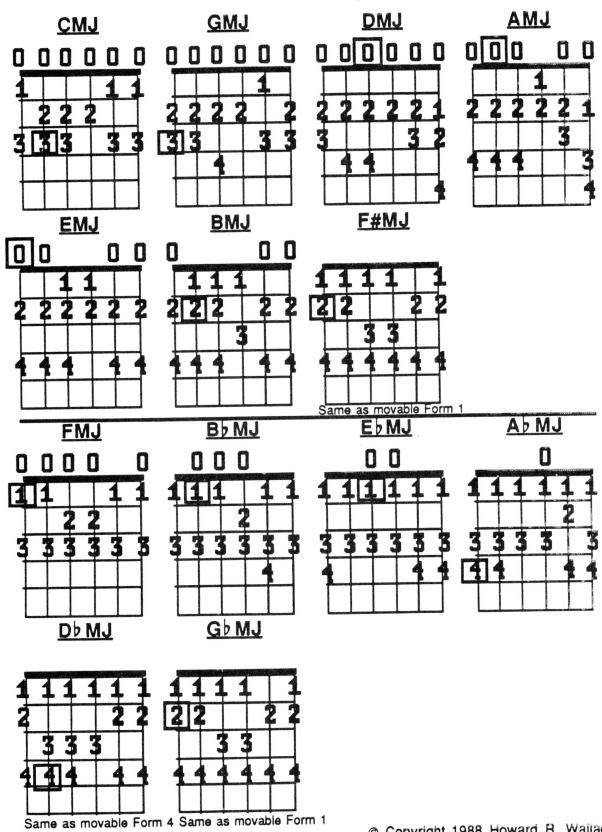

Same as movable Form 1

Same as movable Form 4 Same as movable Form 1

Movable Major Scales

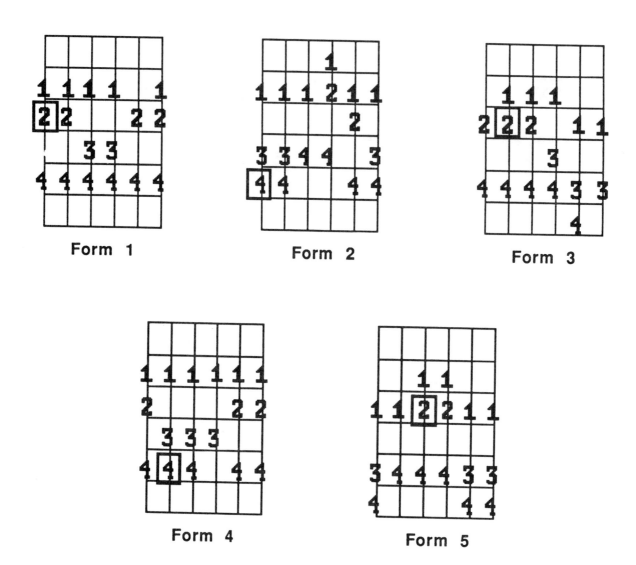

Form 1   Form 2   Form 3

Form 4   Form 5

Long Movable Major Scales

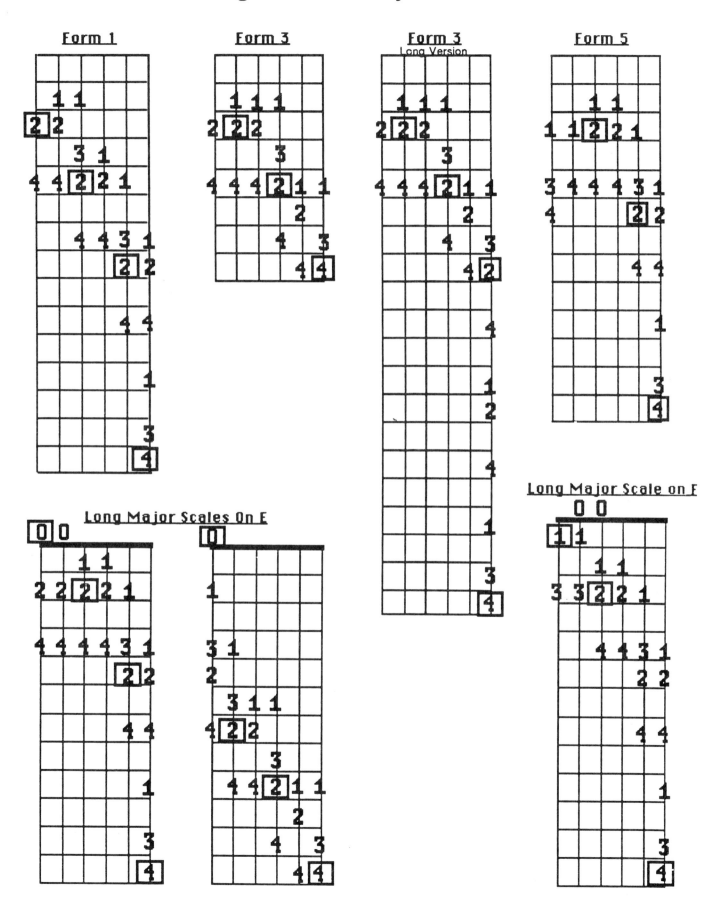

THE MINOR SCALES

Patterns of whole steps and half steps:

Natural Minor

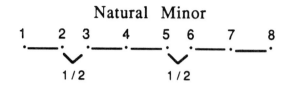

Harmonic Minor

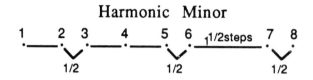

Melodic Minor

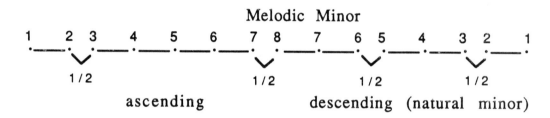

ascending   descending (natural minor)

Jazz Melodic Minor

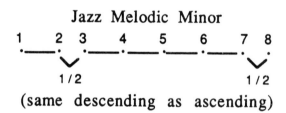

(same descending as ascending)

Hungarian Minor

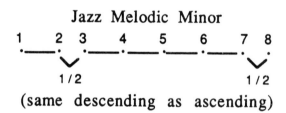

Rumanian

The minor scales are used with (played against) the following kinds of chords:

<u>Natural Minor</u>:

Pure Minor (m)
Minor 7th (m7) that functions as a I, III, or VI
Minor 11th (m11)

<u>Harmonic Minor</u>:

Pure Minor (m)
Minor/Major 7th (m/MJ7)
[also called Minor ♯7th (m♯7)]

<u>Melodic Minor</u>:

Pure Minor (m)

<u>Jazz Melodic Minor</u>:

Pure Minor (m)
Minor 6th (m6)
Minor 6/9 (m6/9)
Minor/Major 7th (m/M7 or m♯7)
          used with ascending scale only
Dominant 9th (Dom 9)
Dominant 13th (Dom 13)

There are also two special ways in which the jazz melodic minor scale is used:

TYPE 1

When you play against a DOMINANT SEVENTH (or Dominant 9th or dominant 13th) CHORD that does NOT resolve down a fifth, use the jazz melodic minor scale that begins on the tonic a FIFTH HIGHER than the root of the chord. For example: G Dominant 7th, use jazz melodic minor scale starting on D. Another example: C Dominant 7th, use jazz melodic minor starting on G.

TYPE 2

When you play against a DOMINANT SEVENTH (or Dominant 9th or dominant 13th) CHORD that DOES resolve down a fifth, use the jazz melodic minor scale that begins on the tonic a HALF STEP HIGHER than the root of the chord. For example: G Dominant 7th, use jazz melodic minor scale on Ab. Another example: C Dominant 7th, use jazz melodic scale on Db.

Hungarian Minor:

Pure Minor (m)
Minor/Major 7th (m/MJ7)
[also called Minor ♯7 (m♯7)]

Rumanian Minor:

Pure minor (m)
Minor 7th (m7)

All long movable minor scale patterns begin with the first finger. Included is a version for each scale type beginning on the open E string. You will see that alternate fingerings are given for the long movable natural minor scale. The two fingerings are equally good. The choice is yours.

For the melodic minor scales, begin with the ascending pattern until you reach the highest note. Then follow the arrow to the appropriate note on the descending scale and from there, play down to the lowest note. If that note is not the tonic then play back up again until you reach the tonic.

For improvisation the Hungarian and Rumanian minor scales are an interesting alternative to the more common harmonic and melodic minor scales.

First Position Natural Minor Scales

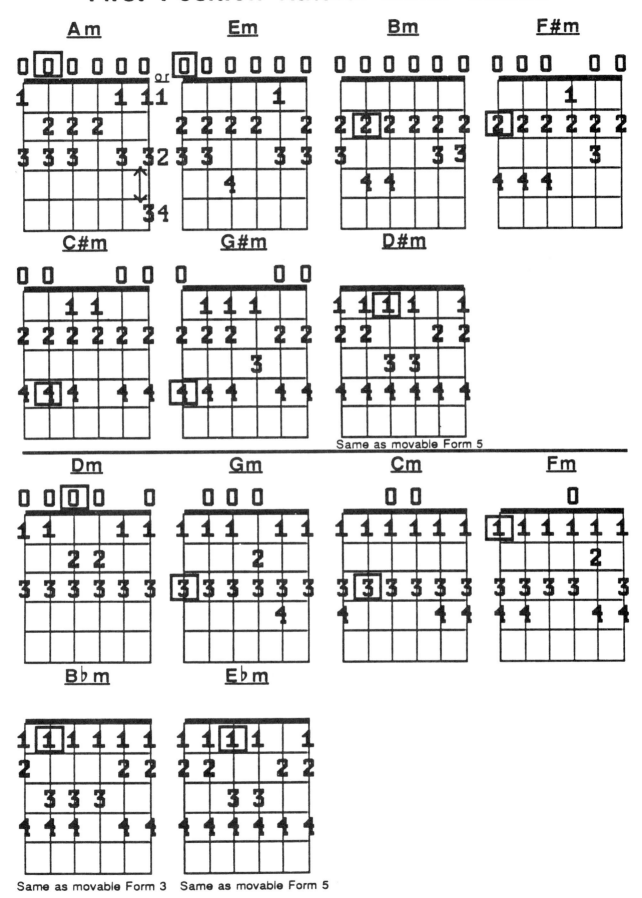

Movable Natural Minor Scales

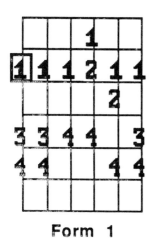

Form 1

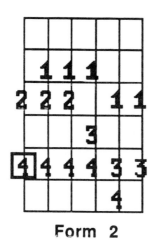

Form 2

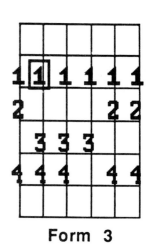

Form 3

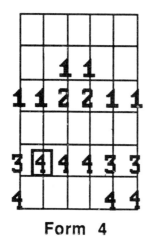

Form 4

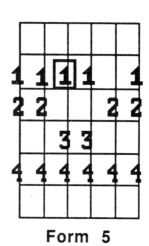

Form 5

Long Movable Natural Minor Scales

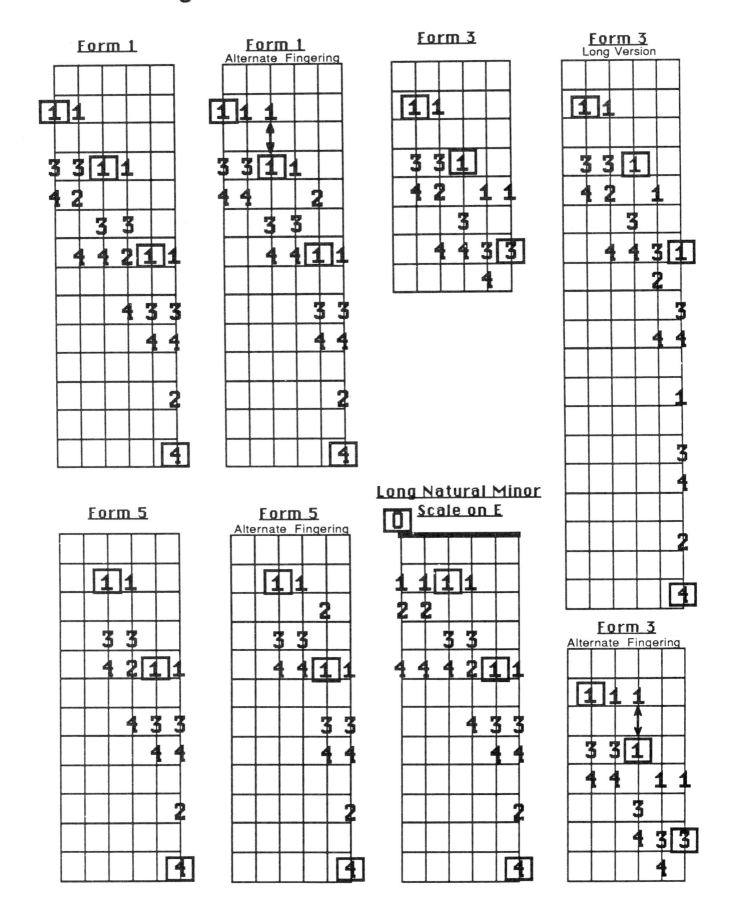

First Position Harmonic Minor Scales

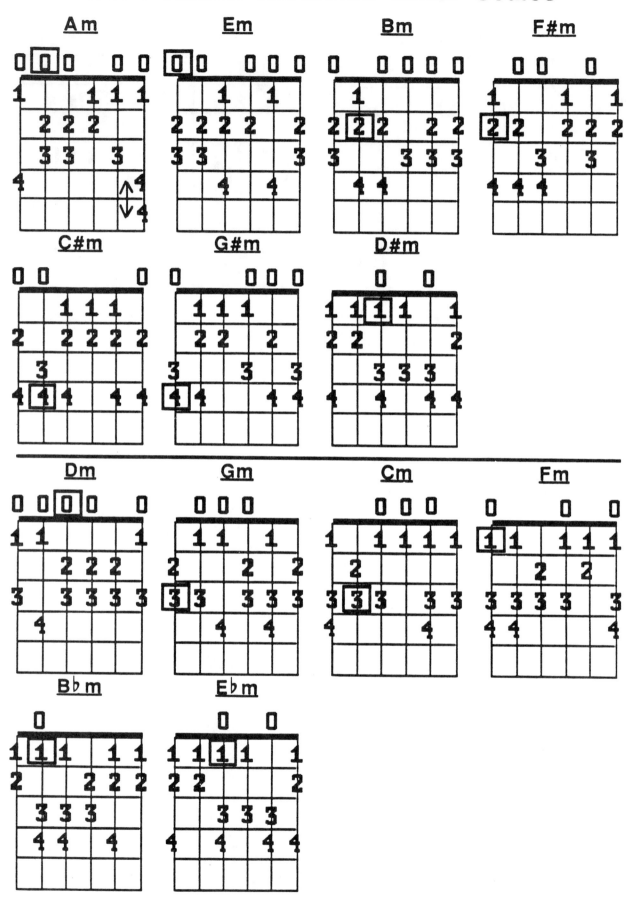

Movable Harmonic Minor Scales

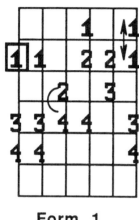

Form 1

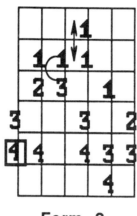

Form 2

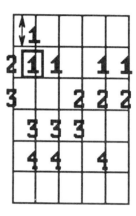

Form 3

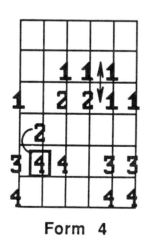

Form 4

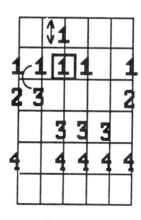

Form 5

19

Long Movable Harmonic Minor Scales

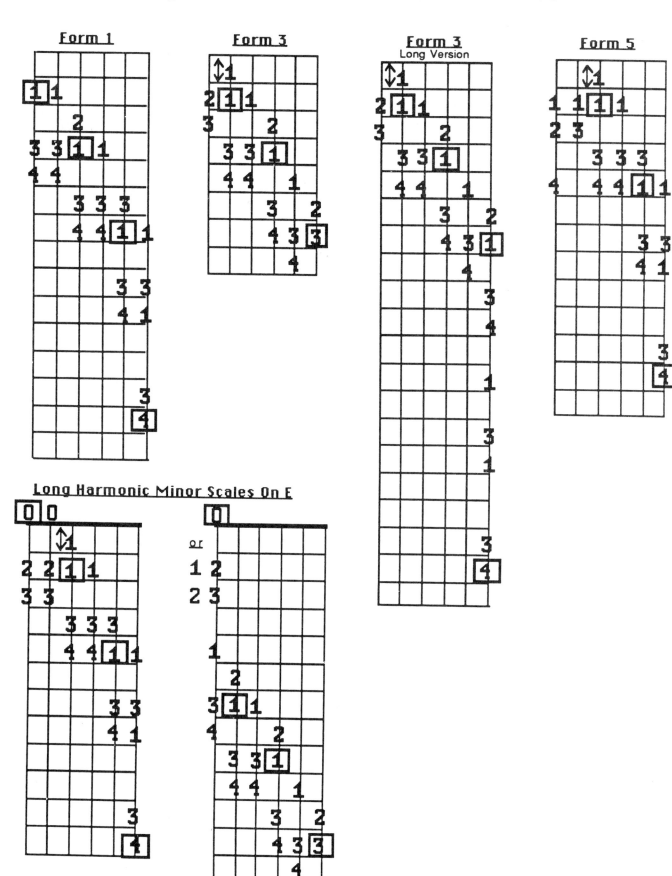

Form 1 Form 3 Form 3 Long Version Form 5

Long Harmonic Minor Scales On E

or

First Position Melodic Minor Scales

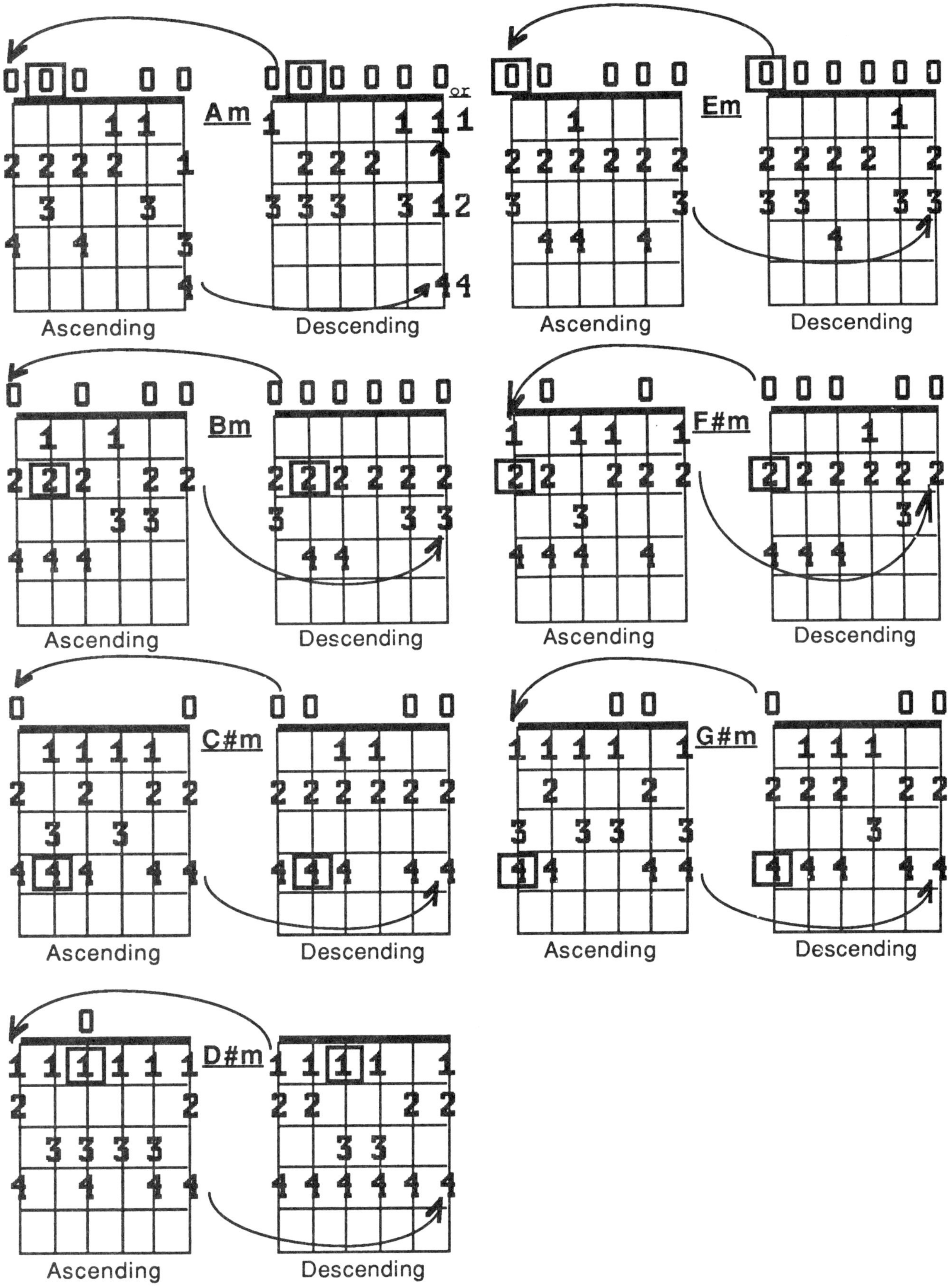

Am — Ascending / Descending or

Em — Ascending / Descending

Bm — Ascending / Descending

F#m — Ascending / Descending

C#m — Ascending / Descending

G#m — Ascending / Descending

D#m — Ascending / Descending

First Position Melodic Minor Scales

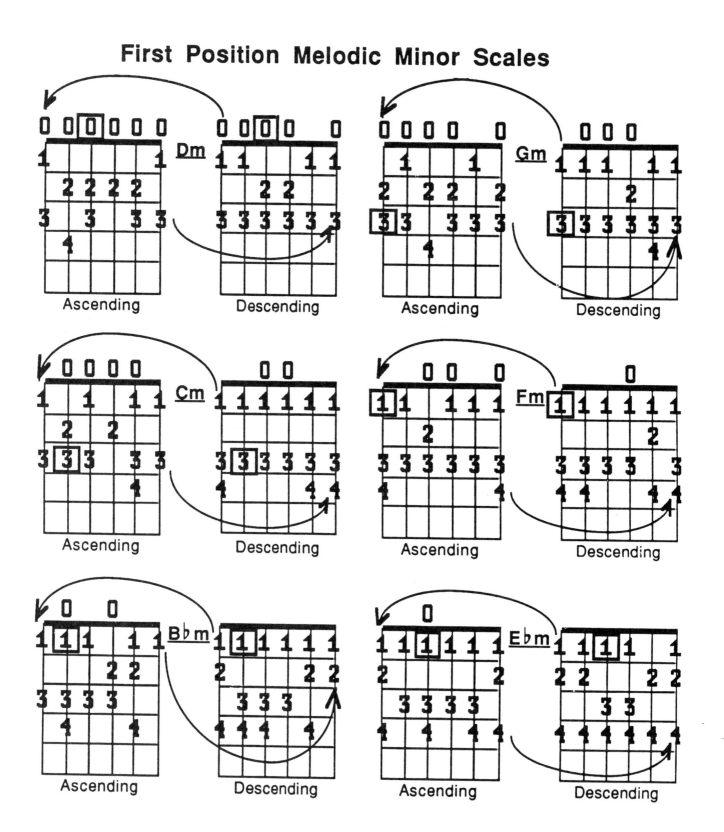

Movable Melodic Minor Scales

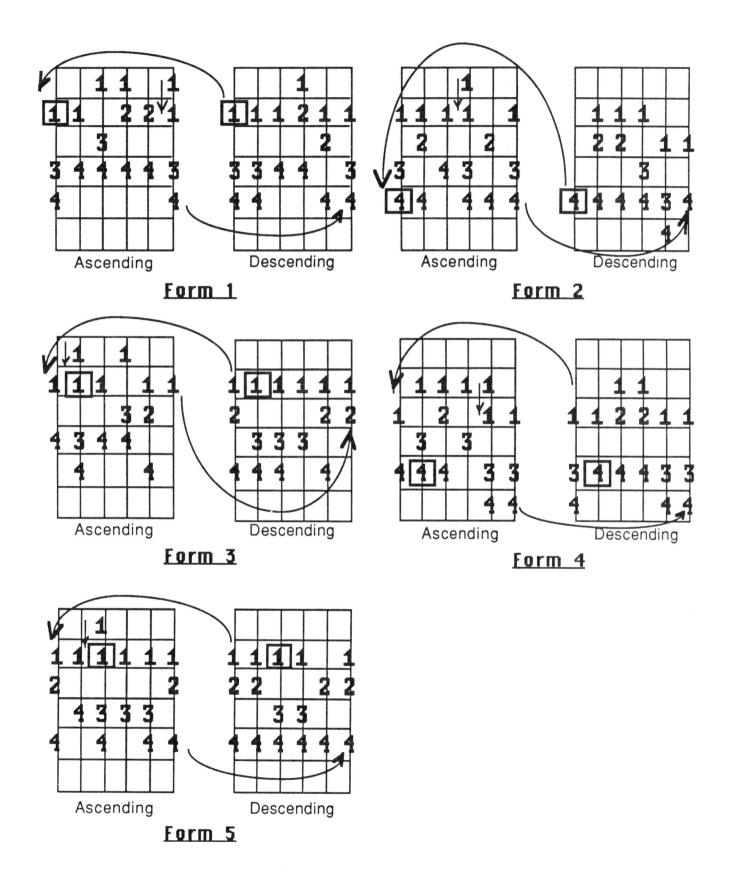

Ascending — Descending

Form 1

Ascending — Descending

Form 2

Ascending — Descending

Form 3

Ascending — Descending

Form 4

Ascending — Descending

Form 5

23

Long Movable Melodic Minor Scales

For Upper Positions On Classical Guitars

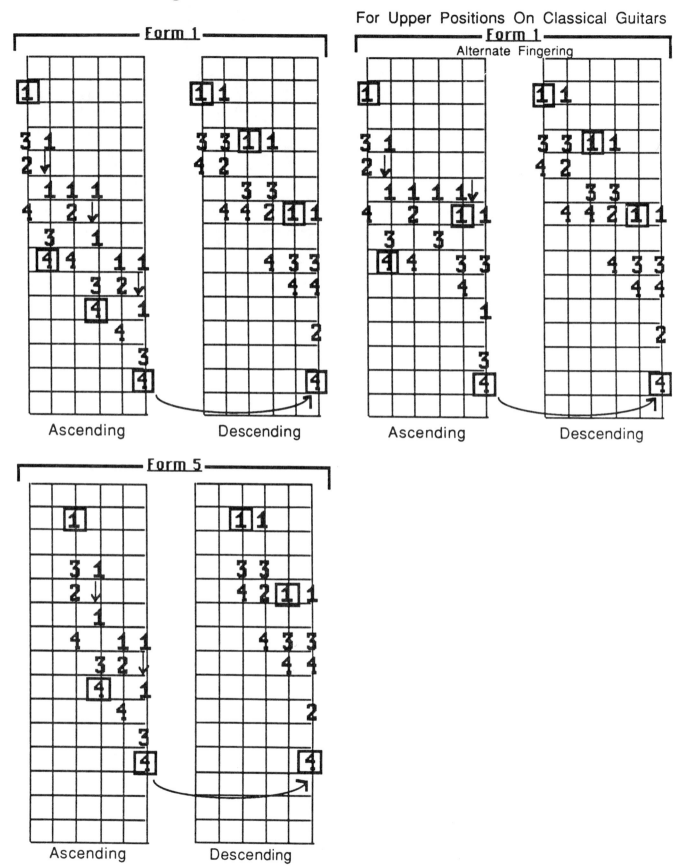

Long Movable Melodic Minor Scales

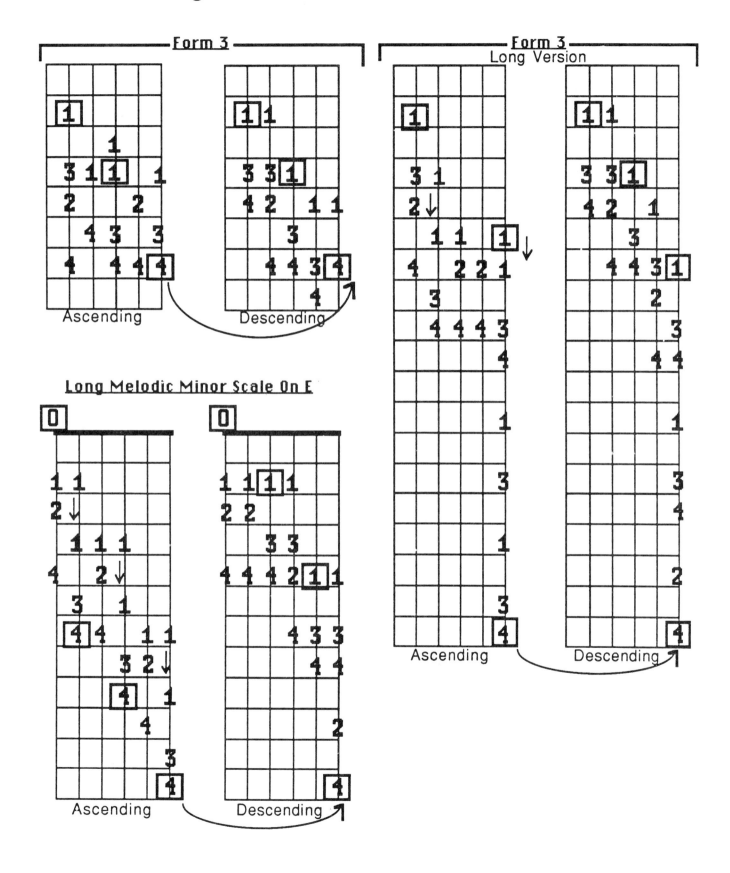

First Position Jazz Melodic Minor Scales

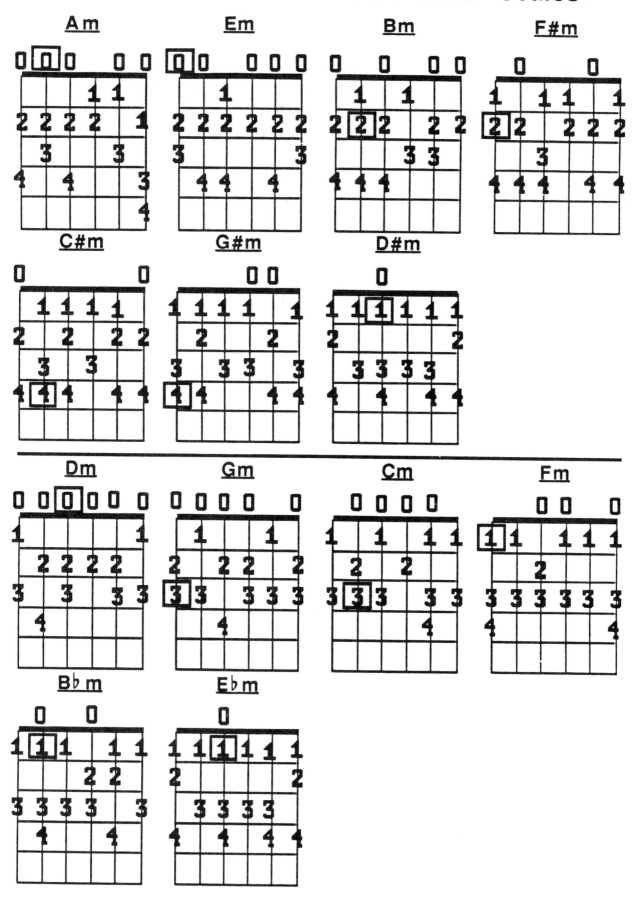

26

Movable Jazz Melodic Minor Scales

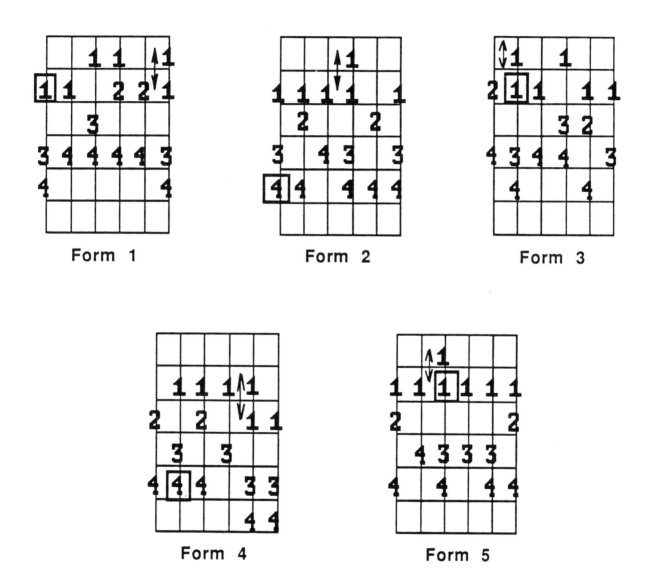

Form 1 Form 2 Form 3

Form 4 Form 5

Long Movable Jazz Melodic Minor Scales

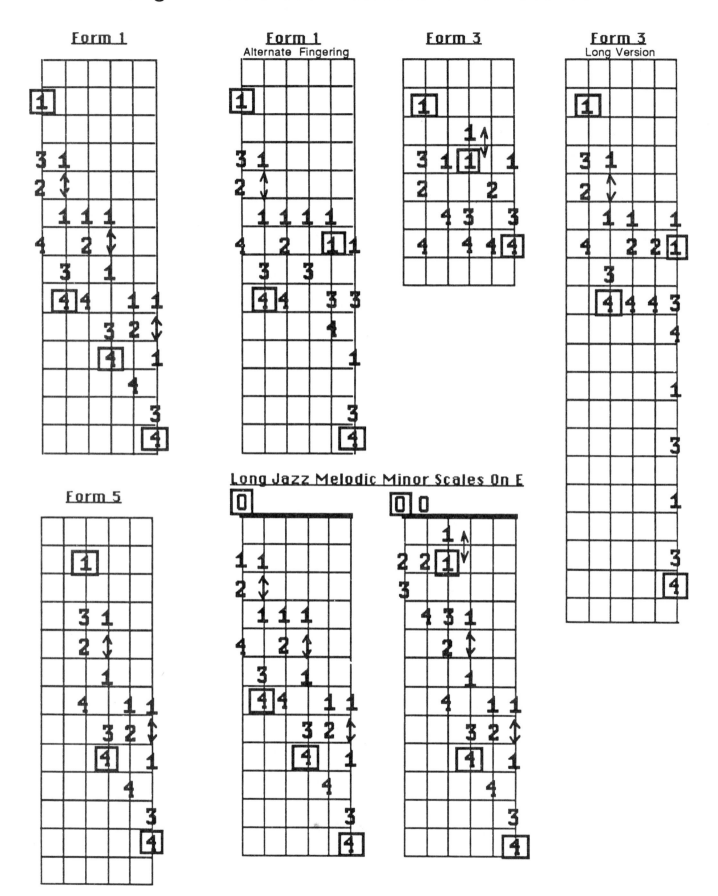

First Position Hungarian Minor Scales

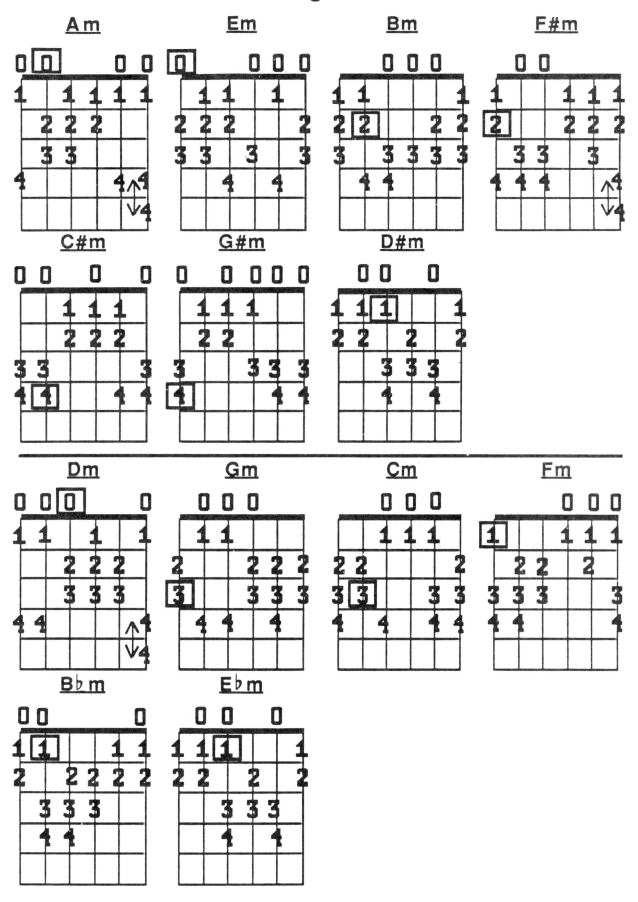

Movable Hungarian Minor Scales

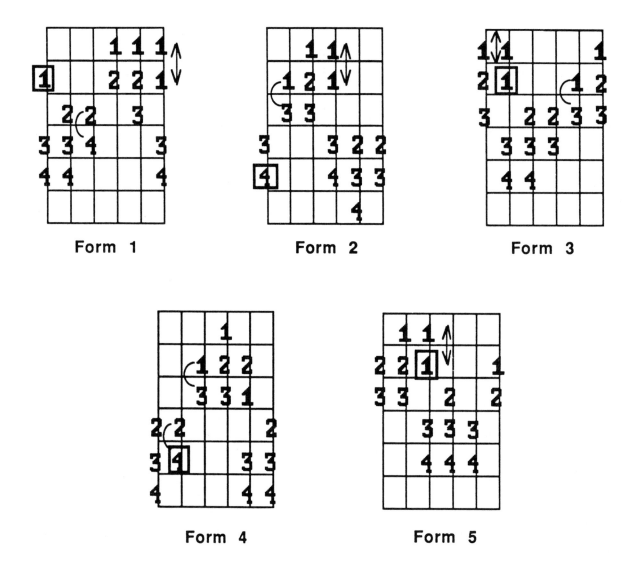

Form 1 Form 2 Form 3

Form 4 Form 5

30

Long Movable Hungarian Minor Scales

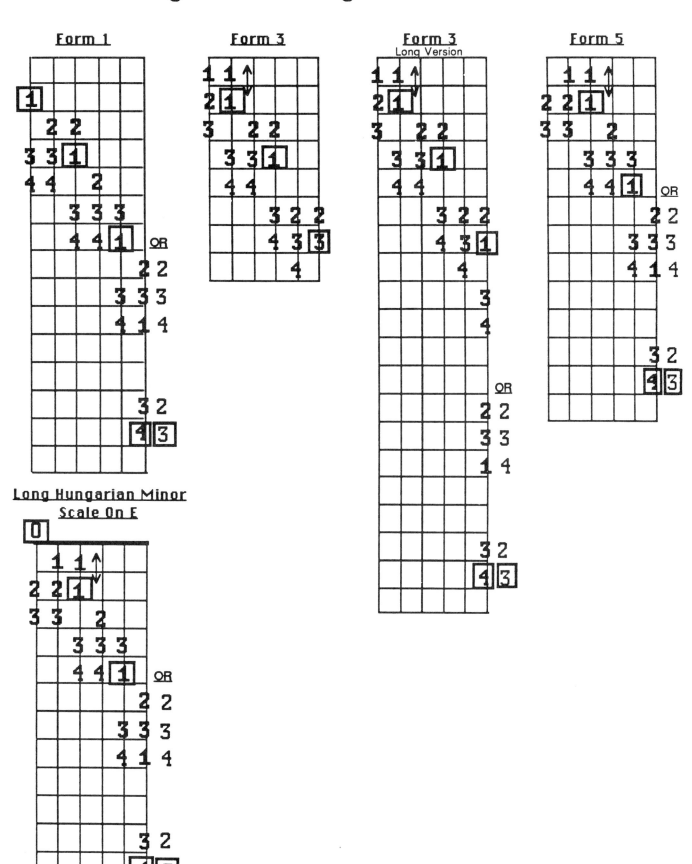

First Position Rumanian Minor Scales

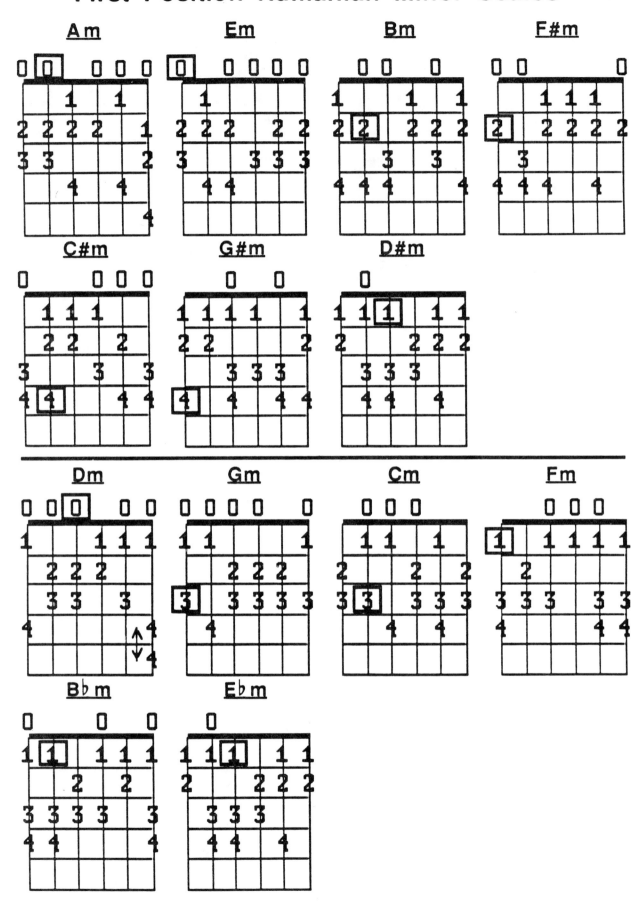

Movable Rumanian Minor Scales

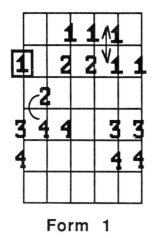

Form 1

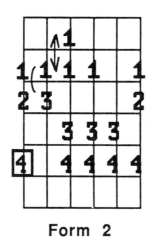

Form 2

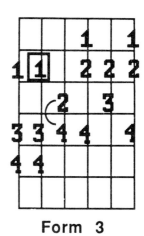

Form 3

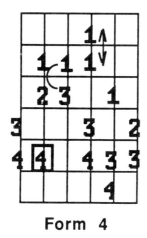

Form 4

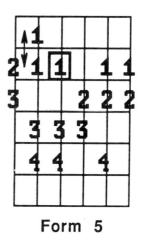

Form 5

33

D235

Long Movable Rumanian Minor Scales

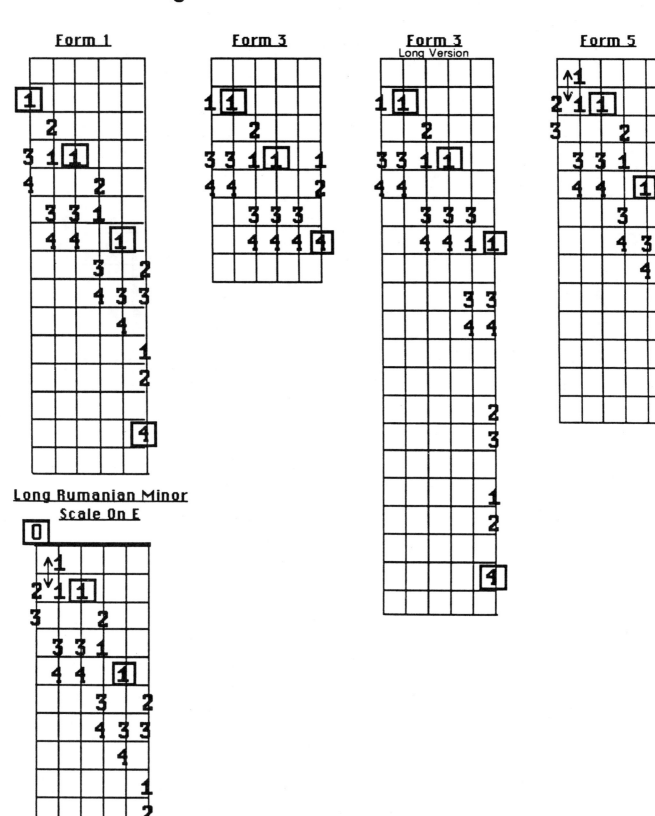

The Complete Book of Scales and Arpeggios In Tablature For The Guitar

The Pentatonic Scales And The Modes

THE PENTATONIC SCALES

Patterns of whole steps and half steps:

Below are the patterns of half steps and whole steps of the pentatonic scales. The straight line indicates whole steps, the "v" shaped symbol indicates the half steps.

The pentatonic scales contain five notes. The minor pentatonic blues scale contains an added raised third scale degree. The sixth tone indicated below is a repeat of the tonic.

Major Pentatonic

1 ___ 2 ___ 3 ₁1/2steps 4 ___ 5 ₁1/2steps 6

Minor Pentatonic

1 ₁1/2steps 2 ___ 3 ___ 4 ₁1/2steps 5 ___ 6

Minor Pentatonic Blues

1 ₁1/2steps 2 ___ 3 ♯3 4 ₁1/2steps 5 ___ 6

1/2 1/2

The pentatonic scales are used with (played against) the following kinds of chords:

Major Pentatonic:
Pure Major (MJ)
Major 6/9 (MJ6/9)
Dominant 7th (Dom 7)
Dominant 7th (Dom 7) from a whole step below the root of the chord
Dominant 7th (Dom 7) with altered 5th and 9th, begin scale on flatted 5th of chord

Minor Pentatonic:
Pure Minor (m)
Minor 7th (m7)
Minor 7th that functions as a II (supertonic)
Minor 7th with suspended 4th (m7 sus4)
Dominant 7th (Dom 7)
Dominant 7th with sharp 9th (Dom 7$\sharp$9)
Dominant 7th with suspended 4th (Dom 7 sus4), begin scale on 5th of chord
Minor 6th (m6)
Minor 6/9 (m6/9)
Dominant 7th (Dom 7) with altered 5th and 9th, begin scale on flatted 3rd of chord
Dominant 9th (Dom 9) begin scale on 5th of chord
Minor 11th (m11)

Minor Pentatonic Blues:
Pure Minor (m)
Minor 7th (m7) that functions as II (supertonic)
Minor 7th with suspended 4th (m7 sus4)
Minor 6th (m6)
Minor 6/9 (m6/9)
Dominant 7th with sharped 9th (Dom 7$\sharp$9)
Dominant 9th (Dom 9) begin scale on 5th of chord

In the minor pentatonic blues scales the numbers in parentheses ( ) indicate the added raised 3rd scale degree - termed "Blue Notes".

The abbreviated versions of the long minor pentatonic blues scales result in a turn of phrase found frequently in rock, blues, and jazz.

First Position Major Pentatonic Scales

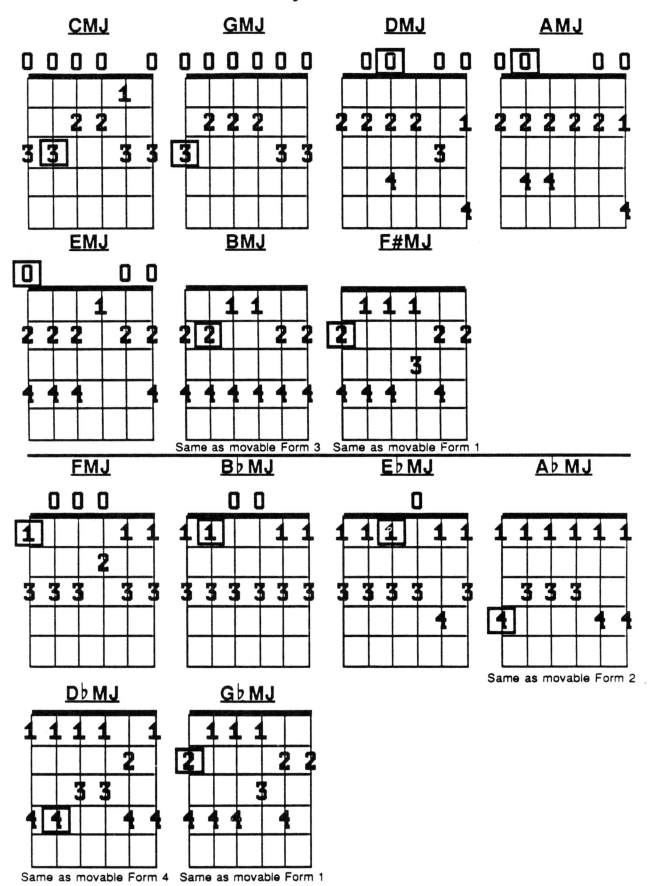

CMJ GMJ DMJ AMJ

EMJ BMJ F#MJ

Same as movable Form 3   Same as movable Form 1

FMJ BbMJ EbMJ AbMJ

Same as movable Form 2

DbMJ GbMJ

Same as movable Form 4   Same as movable Form 1

Movable Major Pentatonic Scales

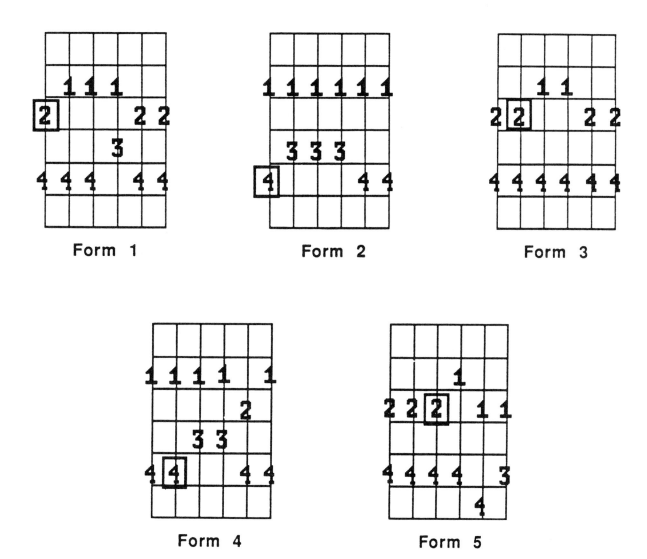

Form 1   Form 2   Form 3

Form 4   Form 5

Long Movable Major Pentatonic Scales

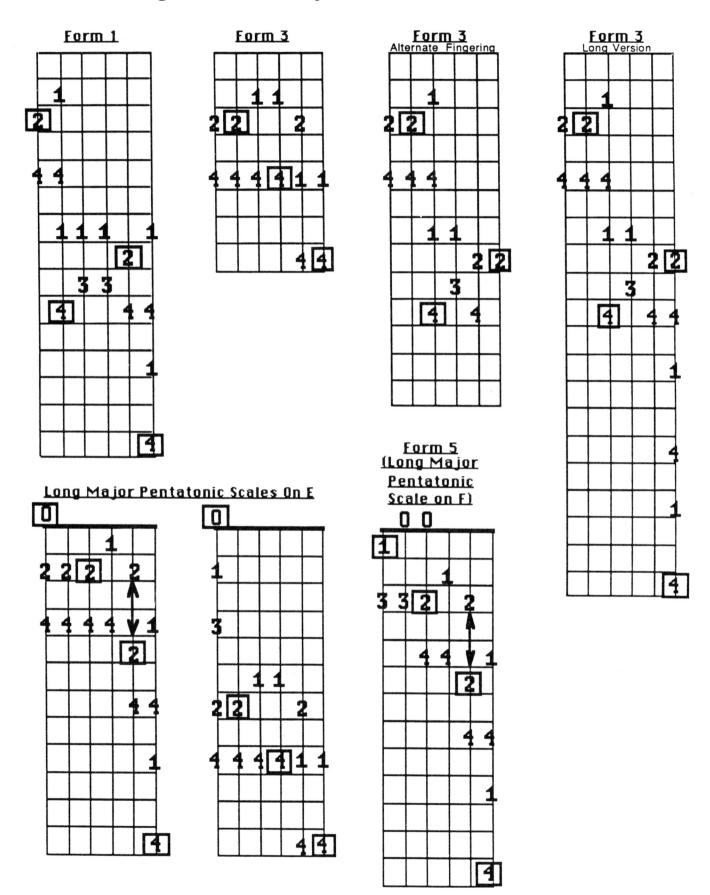

First Position Minor Pentatonic Scales

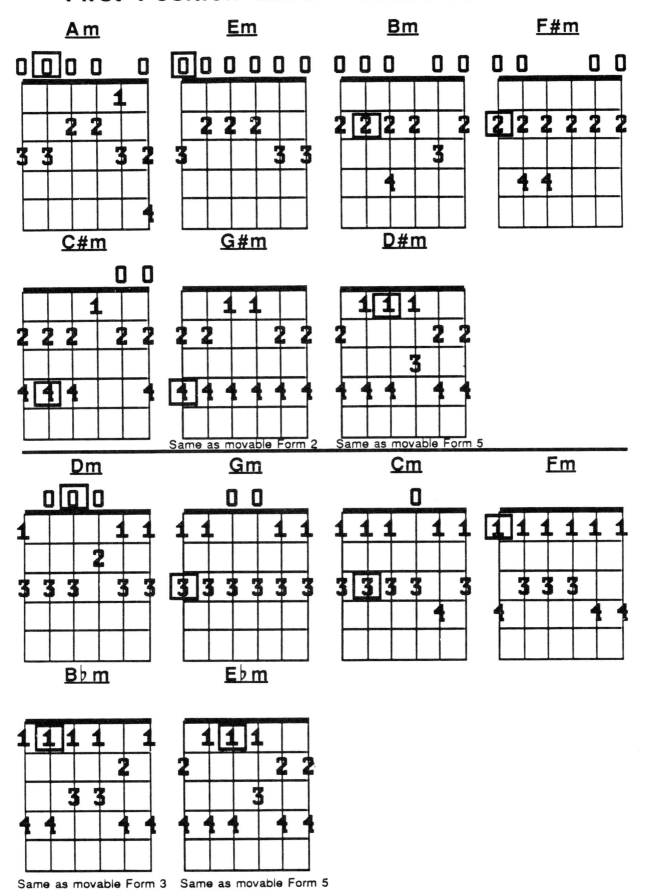

41

Movable Minor Pentatonic Scales

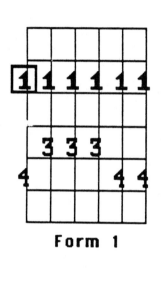

Form 1

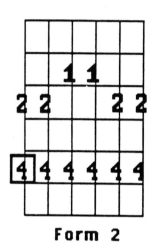

Form 2

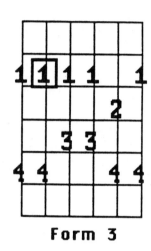

Form 3

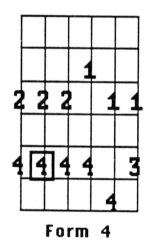

Form 4

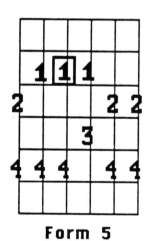

Form 5

Long Movable Minor Pentatonic Scales

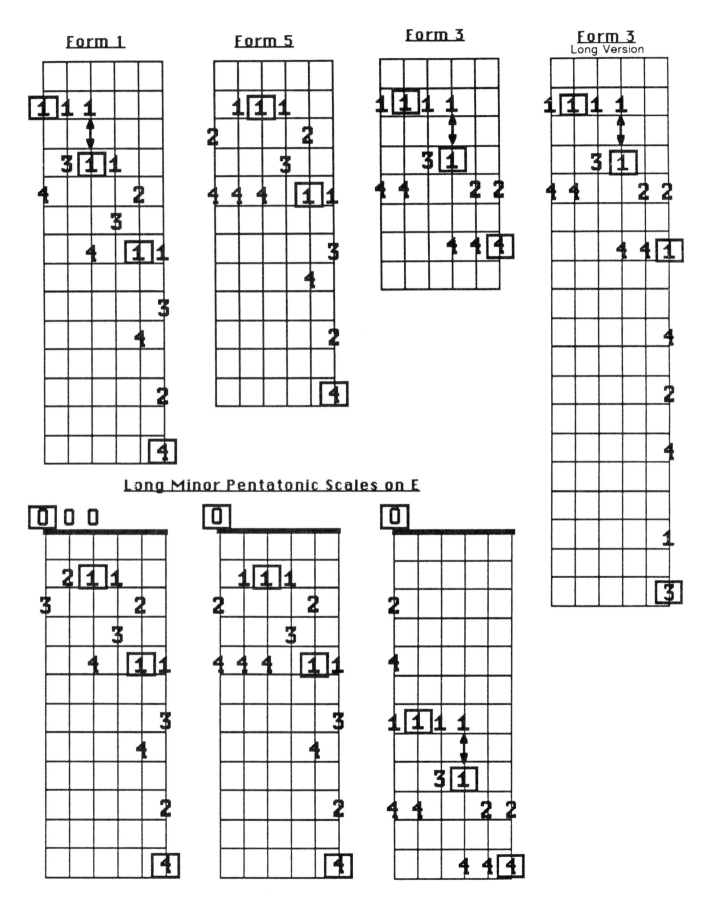

43

First Position Minor Pentatonic Blues Scales

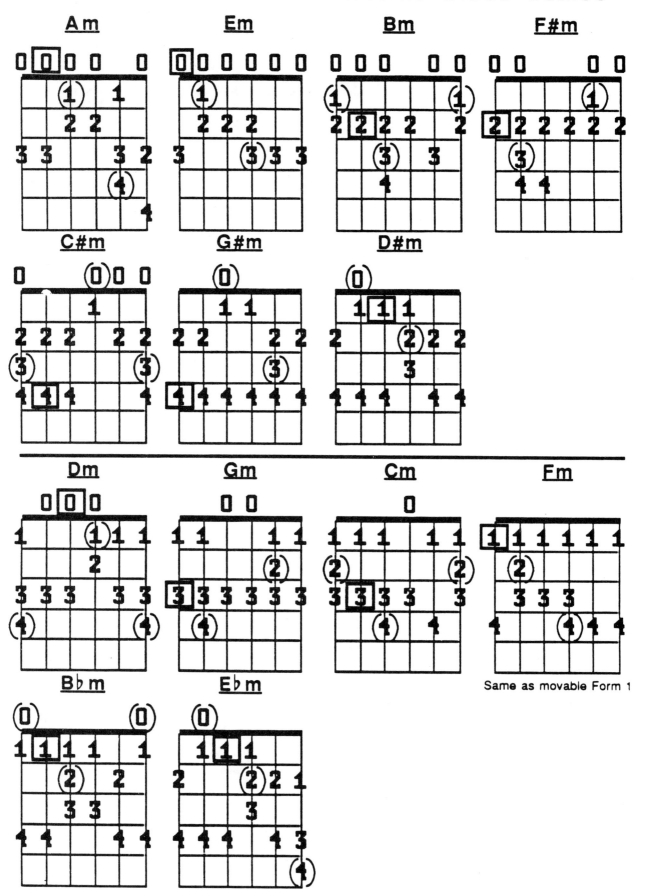

Movable Minor Pentatonic Blues Scales

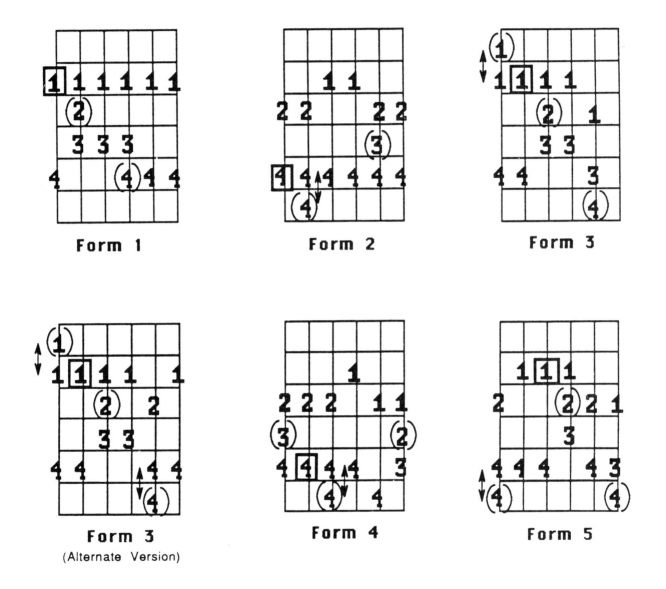

Form 1

Form 2

Form 3

Form 3
(Alternate Version)

Form 4

Form 5

45

Long Movable Minor Pentatonic Blues Scales

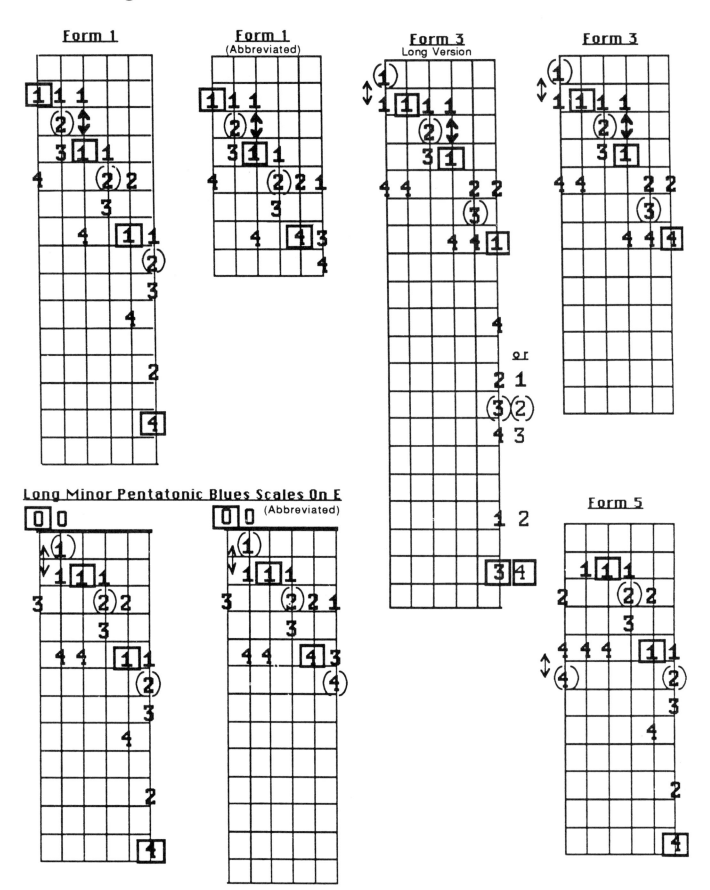

46

THE MODES

Note: There are seven modes: Aeolian, Locrian, Ionian, Dorian, Phrygian, Lydian and Mixolydian. Two of these, the Aeolian and Ionian, are identical to the natural minor and major scales, respectively, which have already been covered.

Patterns of whole steps and half steps:

Locrian

```
1   2       3       4   5       6       7       8
 \_/ _____/ _____
1/2                  1/2
```

Dorian

```
1       2   3       4       5       6   7       8
 _____/ _____/ _____
        1/2                          1/2
```

Phrygian

```
1   2       3       4       5   6       7       8
 \_/ _____/ _____
1/2                          1/2
```

Lydian

```
1       2       3       4   5       6       7   8
 _____/ _____/
                        1/2                  1/2
```

Mixolydian

```
1       2       3   4       5       6   7       8
 _____/ _____/ _____
                1/2                  1/2
```

47

The modes are used with (played against) the following kinds of chords:

Locrian:
Minor 7th with flatted 5th (m7 ♭5)
Half Diminished 7th (1/2dim 7, ø7)
Dominant 9th (Dom 9) begin mode on 3rd of chord

Dorian:
Minor 7th (m7) that functions as II (supertonic)
Minor 7th with suspended 4th (m7 sus4)
Dominant 7th with sharped 9th (Dom7♯9)

Phrygian:
Pure minor (m)
Minor 7th (m7) that functions as I, III or VI

Lydian:
Major 7th (MJ7)
Major 7th with flatted 5th (MJ7 ♭5)
Dominant 7th with flatted 5th (Dom7 ♭5)
Dominant 7th with sharped 11th (Dom7 ♯11)

Mixolydian:
Dominant 7th (Dom7)
Dominant 7th with suspended 4th (Dom7 sus4)
Dominant 9th (Dom9)
Dominant 11th (Dom11)
Dominant 13th (Dom13)

The long movable Phrygian and Mixolydian modes are presented with alternate fingerings. In each case, the alternate version uses the same finger on the tonic (boxed note), which is preferred by many players.

First Position Locrian Mode

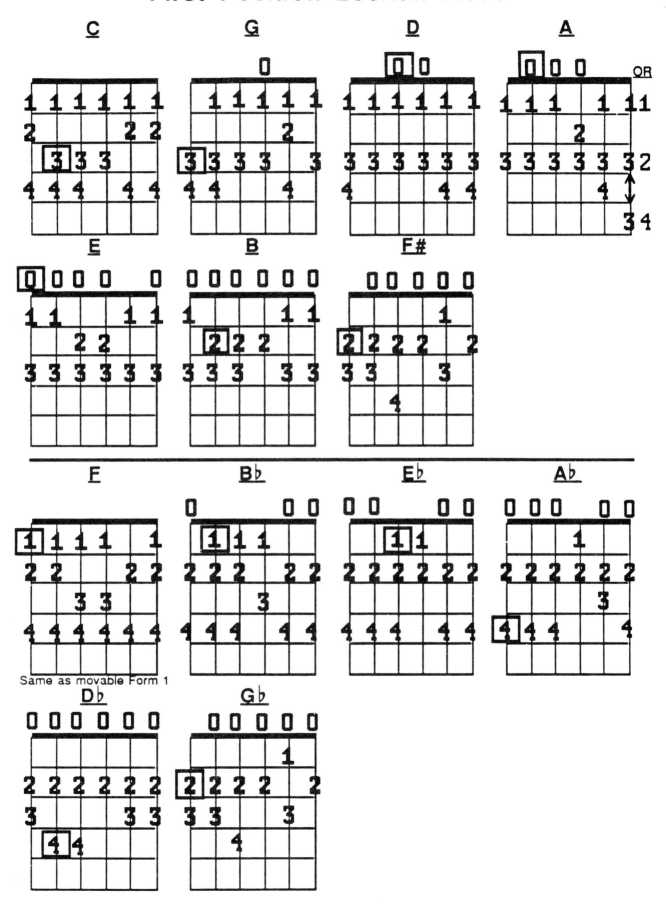

Movable Locrian Mode

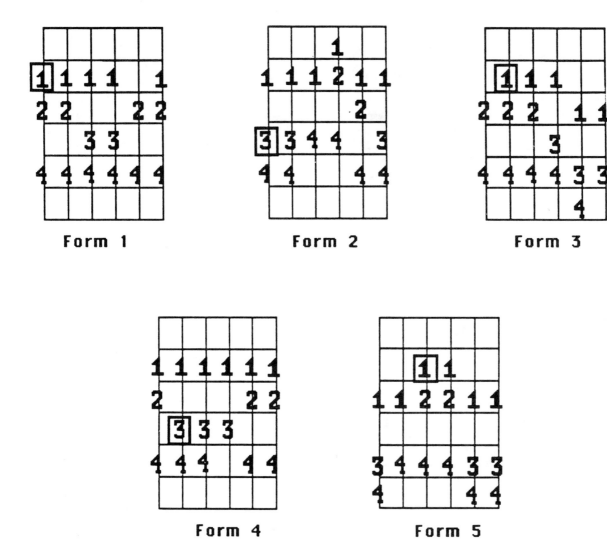

Form 1   Form 2   Form 3

Form 4   Form 5

Long Movable Locrian Mode

Form 1

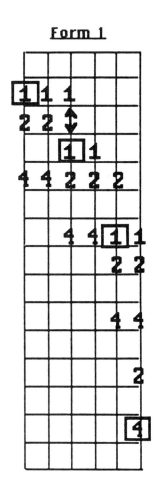

Form 3

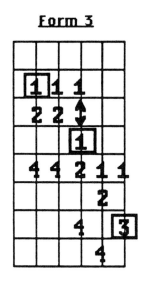

Form 3
Long Version

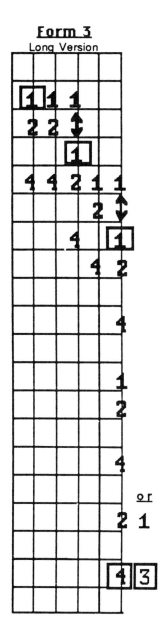

Form 5

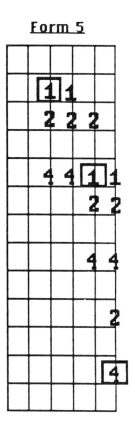

Long Locrian On E

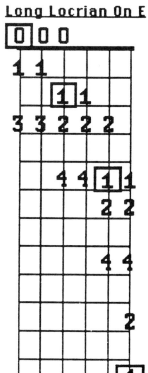

First Position Dorian Mode

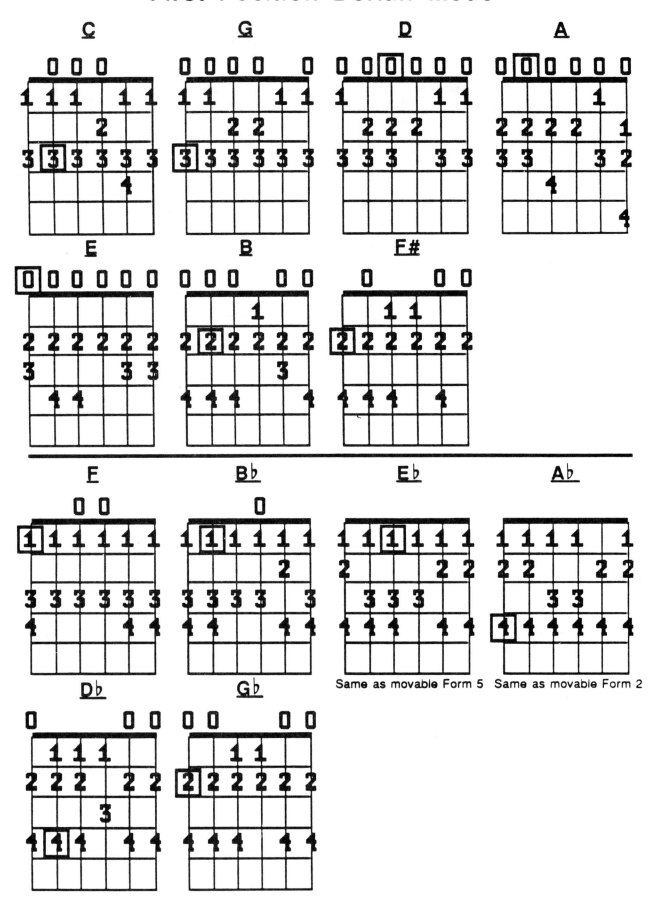

Same as movable Form 5   Same as movable Form 2

Movable Dorian Mode

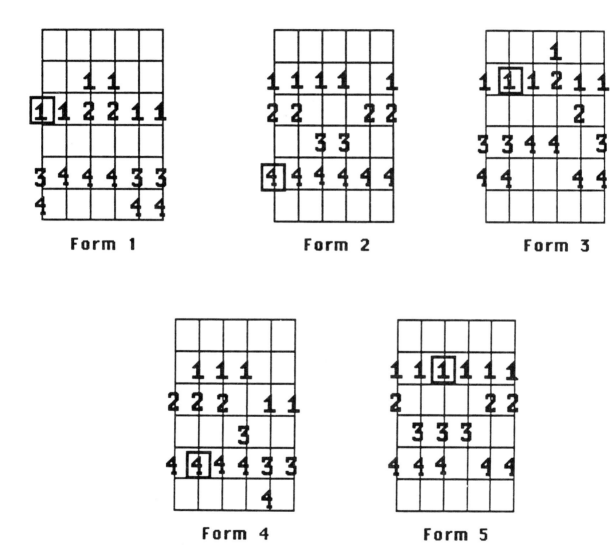

Form 1

Form 2

Form 3

Form 4

Form 5

Long Movable Dorian Mode

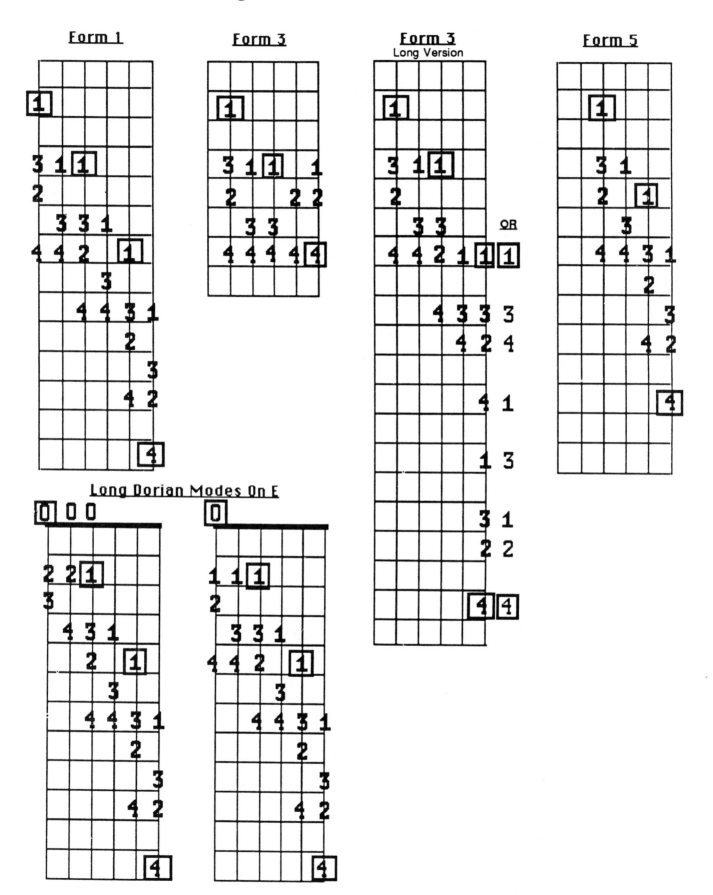

First Position Phrygian Mode

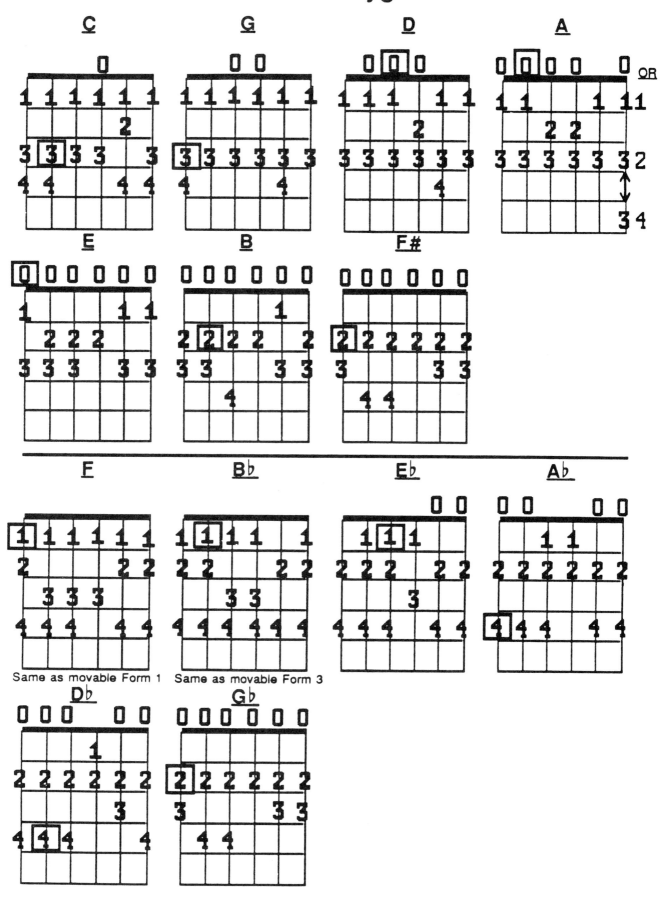

Movable Phrygian Mode

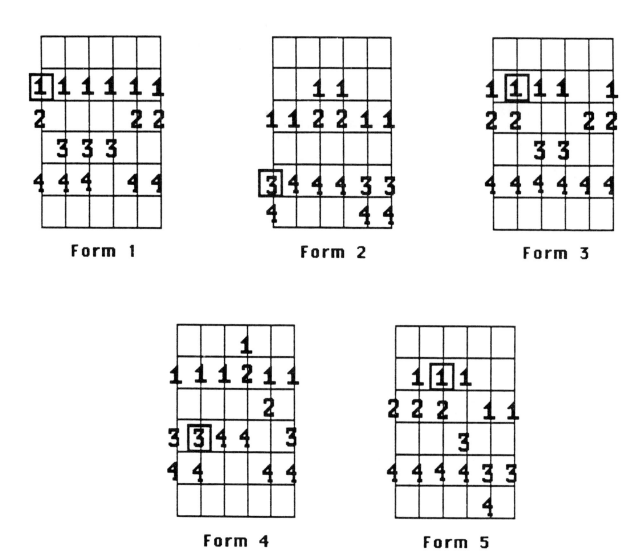

Form 1   Form 2   Form 3

Form 4   Form 5

Long Movable Phrygian Mode

Form 1
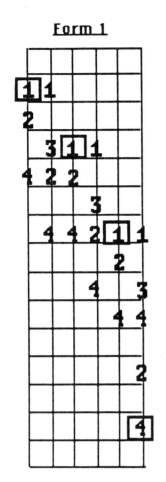

Form 3
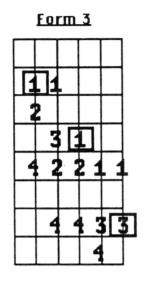

Form 3
Long Version
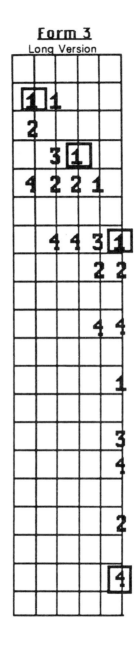

Form 5
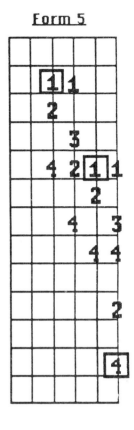

Long Phrygian Mode On E
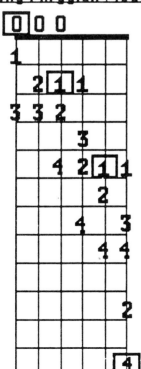

Long Movable Phrygian Mode-Alternate Fingerings

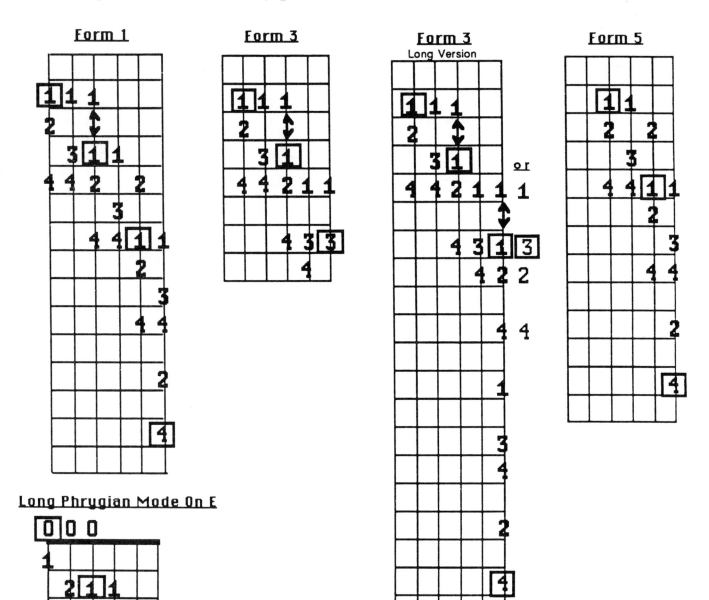

Form 1

Form 3

Form 3
Long Version

Form 5

Long Phrygian Mode On E

58

First Position Lydian Mode

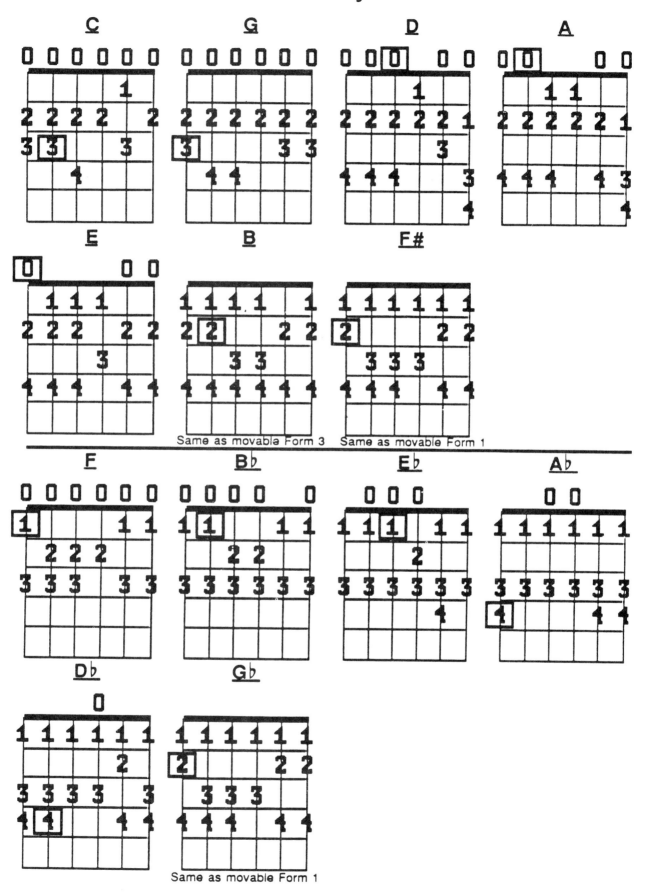

Movable Lydian Mode

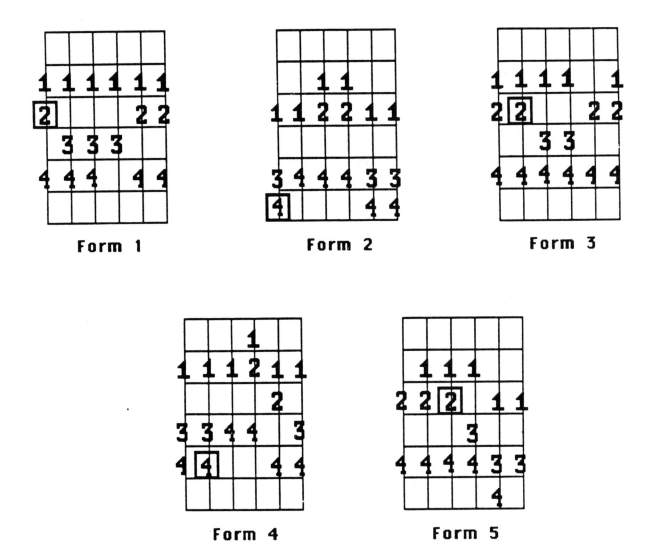

Form 1   Form 2   Form 3

Form 4   Form 5

60

Long Movable Lydian Mode

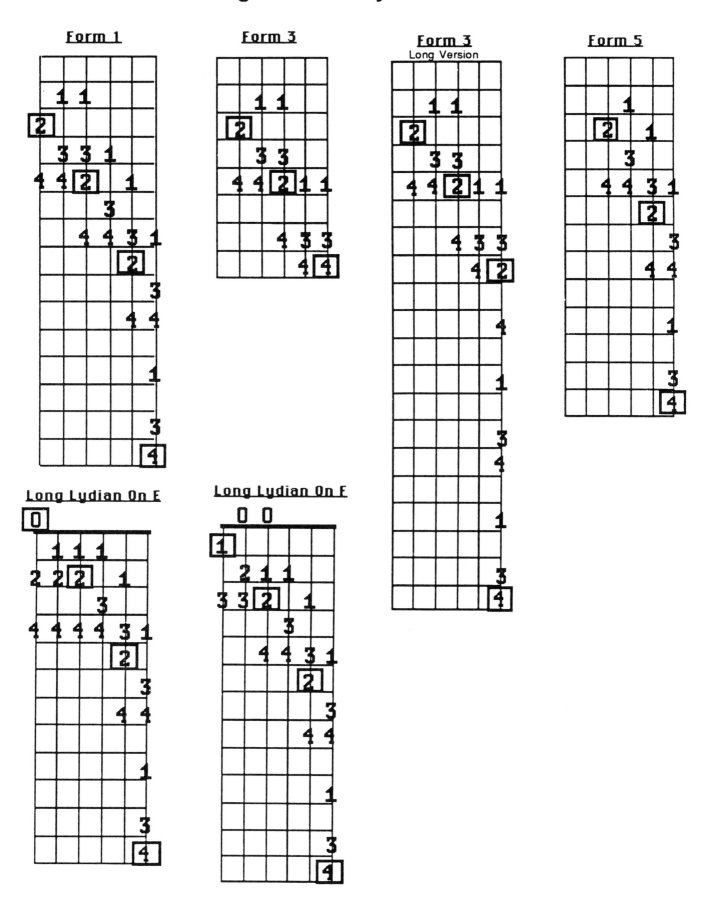

First Position Mixolydian Mode

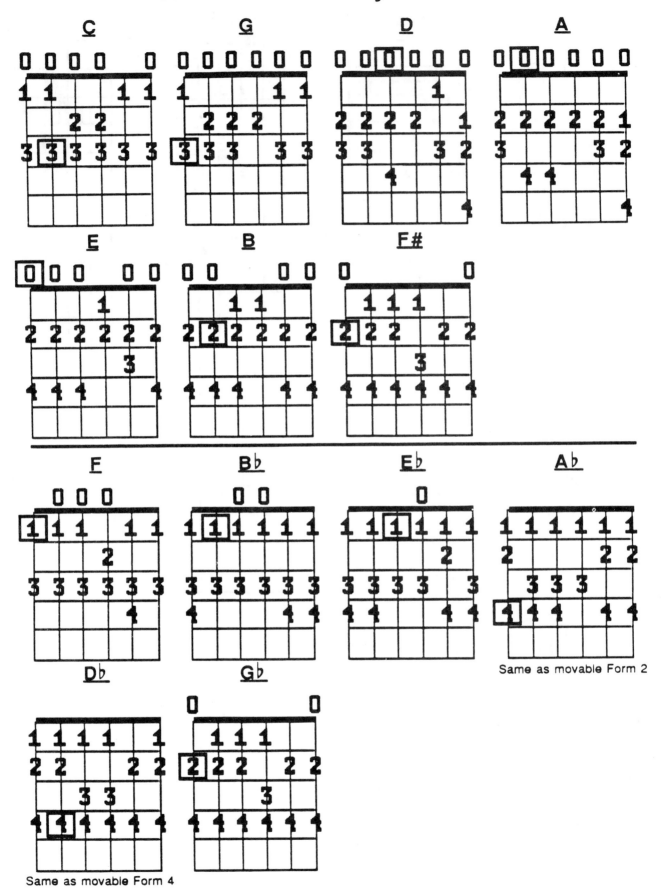

Movable Mixolydian Mode

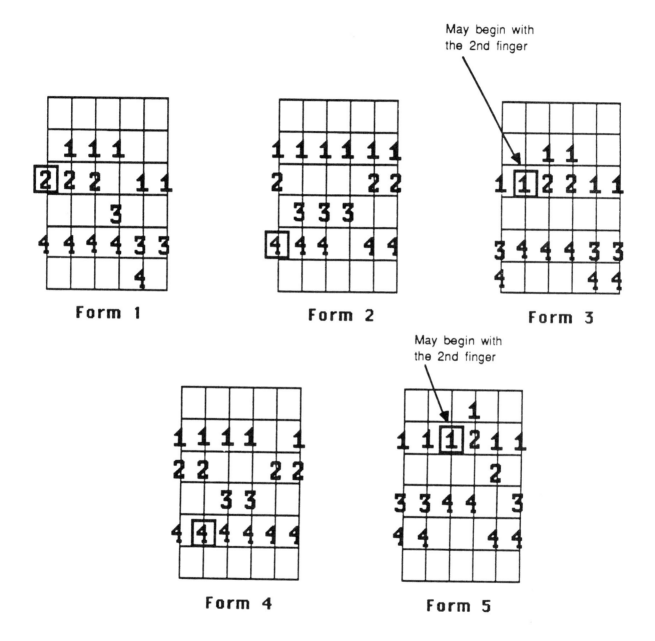

Form 1

Form 2

Form 3
May begin with the 2nd finger

Form 4

Form 5
May begin with the 2nd finger

Long Movable Mixolydian Mode

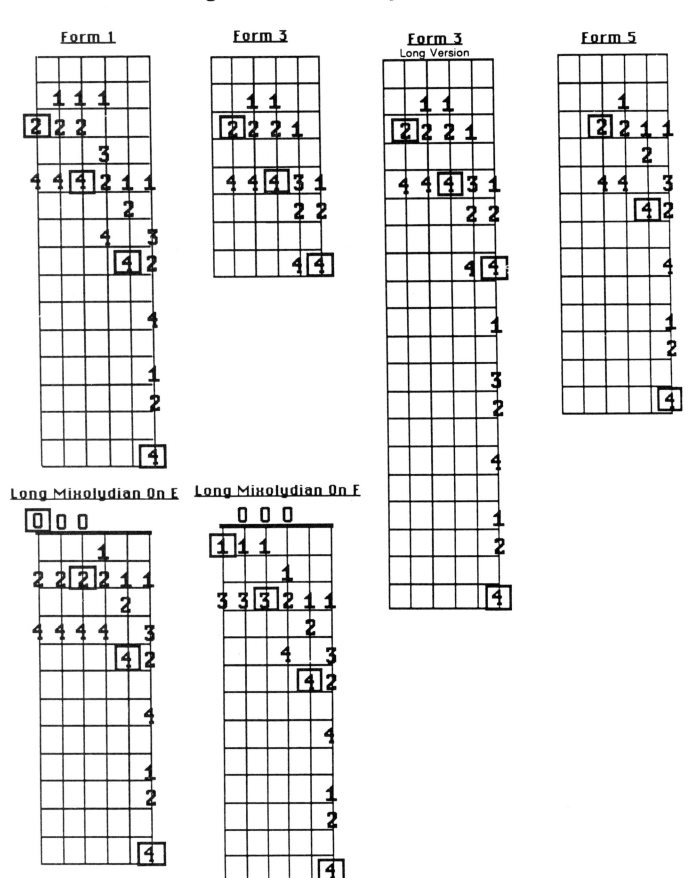

Form 1

Form 3

Form 3
Long Version

Form 5

Long Mixolydian On E

Long Mixolydian On F

64

Long Movable Mixolydian Mode-Alternate Fingerings

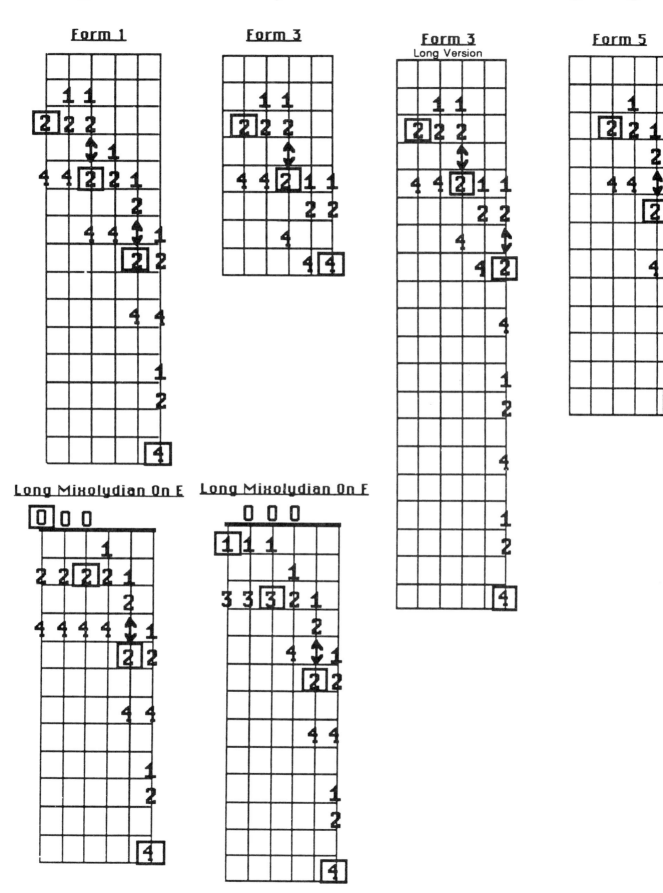

The Complete Book of Scales and Arpeggios In Tablature For The Guitar

Arpeggios And Symmetrical Scales

Part 3

THE SYMMETRICAL SCALES

Patterns of whole steps and half steps:

Below are the patterns of half steps and whole steps of the symmetrical scales. The straight line indicates whole steps, the "v" shaped symbol indicates the half steps.

In symmetrical scales, a single interval or pair of intervals is repeated all the way through. The 9 indicated in the diminished scales, the 7 indicated in the whole tone and augmented scales, and the 13 indicated in the chromatic scale are all repeats of the tonic.

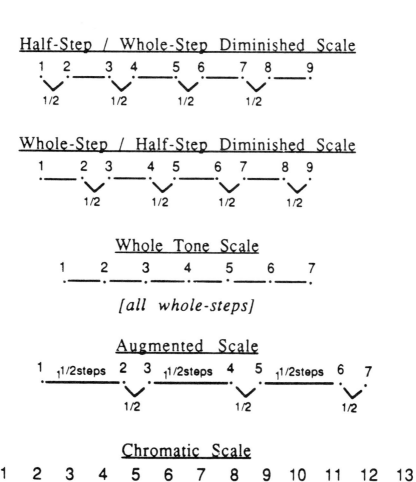

The symmetrical scales are used with (played against) the following kinds of chords:

Half-Step/Whole-Step Diminished Scale:
Dominant 7th with flatted 9th (Dom7 ♭9)
Dominant 7th with sharped 9th (Dom7 ♯9)
Dominant 13th with flatted 9th (Dom13 ♭9)
Dominant 13th with sharped 9th (Dom13 ♯9)

Whole-Step/Half-Step Diminished Scale:
Diminished 7th (dim7 or °7)
Half-Diminished 7th (ø7) also known as Minor 7th with flatted 5th (m7 ♭5)
Minor 7th that functions as II (supertonic)

Whole Tone Scale:
Augmented (Aug. or +)
Dominant 7th with flatted 5th (Dom7 ♭5)
Dominant 7th with sharped 5th (Dom7 ♯5)
Dominant 9th with sharped 11th (Dom9 ♯11)

Augmented Scales:
Augmented (Aug. or +)
Major 7th with sharped 5th (MJ7 ♯5)

Chromatic Scale:
All chords*

*NOTE: Because the chromatic scale contains every note, it can be played against any type of chord with any combination of chordal alterations. However, it should be used sparingly and in good taste.

In the movable half-step/whole-step and whole-step/half-step diminished scale pages, there are two basic fingering patterns broken down into Form A and Form B, depending upon which finger you use to start the scale. These forms indicate all the possible tonic positions. Each tablature block contains the scale with the tonic on the sixth, fifth, fourth, and third string. They maintain their shape (pattern) regardless of which string on which you begin.

In the movable whole-tone scales, the alternate fingering provided for the scale that begins with the tonic on the sixth string may also be used for the scales which begin on the fifth and fourth strings. The three fingerings (Type 3) given at the bottom of the page are quite difficult and should be used only after the left hand is well developed and stretching no longer poses a physical problem.

In the chromatic scales, note that no boxes are provided to indicate the tonic. This is because any note in the chromatic scale may be considered a tonic. Consequently, the scale can be played starting with any finger anywhere on the fingerboard.

The extra long movable chromatic scale can be played as high as access on your guitar allows. If played to the highest note indicated, they require a guitar fingerboard with 24 frets.

First Position Half Step/Whole Step Diminished Scales

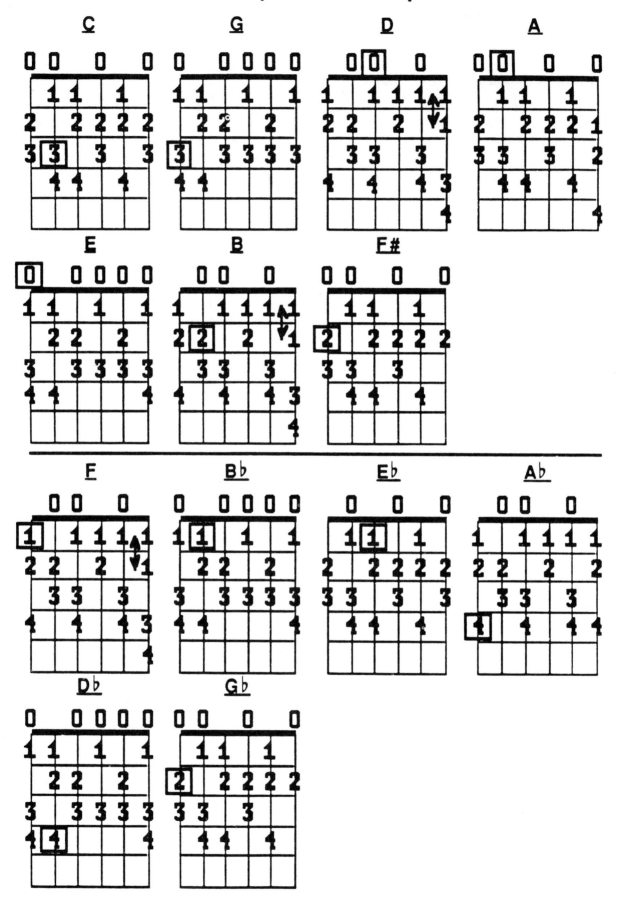

70

Movable Half Step/Whole Step Diminished Scales

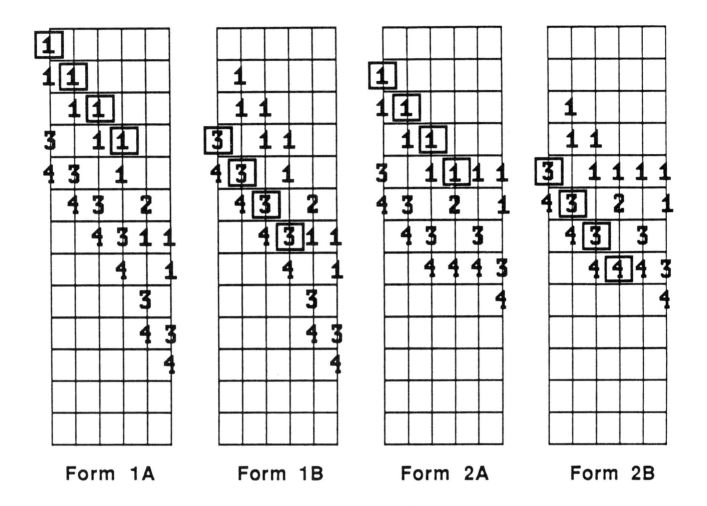

Form 1A   Form 1B   Form 2A   Form 2B

• Each of the above tablature blocks contains four separate half step / whole step diminished scales.

• Each tonic box indicates a separate starting note for each of those four scales.

• Practice each tablature block by first playing the scale starting on the boxed tonic on the 6th string, then on the 5th string, then on the 4th string, and finally on the 3rd string.

First Position Whole Step/Half Step Diminished Scales

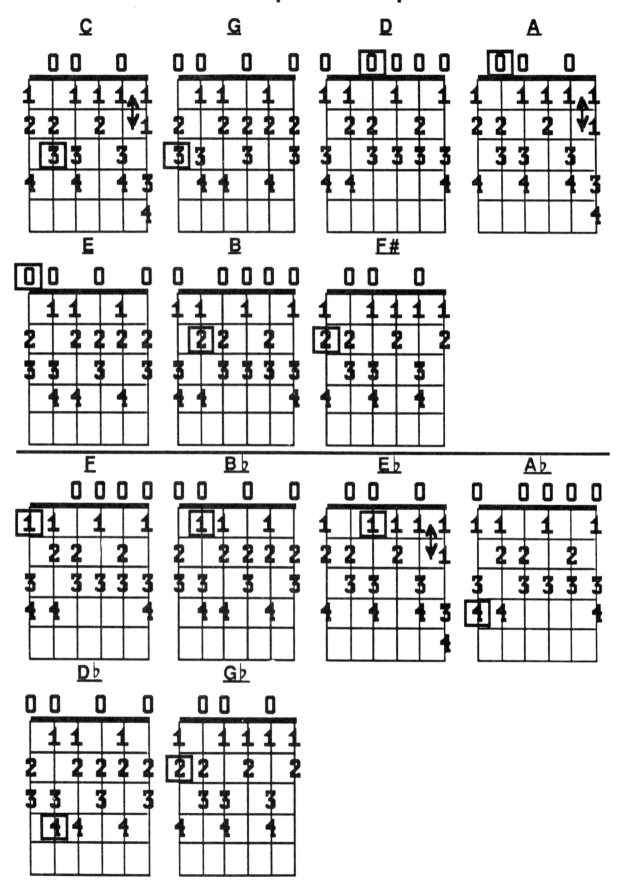

Movable Whole Step/Half Step Diminished Scales

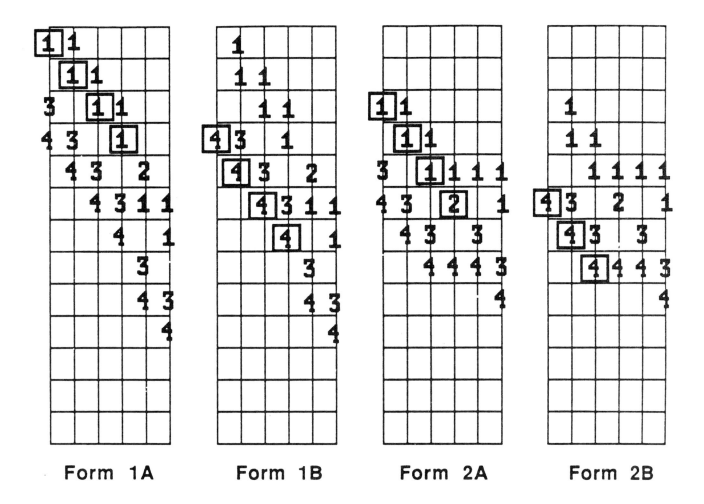

Form 1A   Form 1B   Form 2A   Form 2B

- Each of the above tablature blocks contains four separate whole step / half step diminished scales.

- Each tonic box indicates a separate starting note for each of those four scales.

- Practice each tablature block by first playing the scale starting on the boxed tonic on the 6th string, then on the 5th string, then on the 4th string, and finally on the 3rd string.

First Position Whole Tone Scales

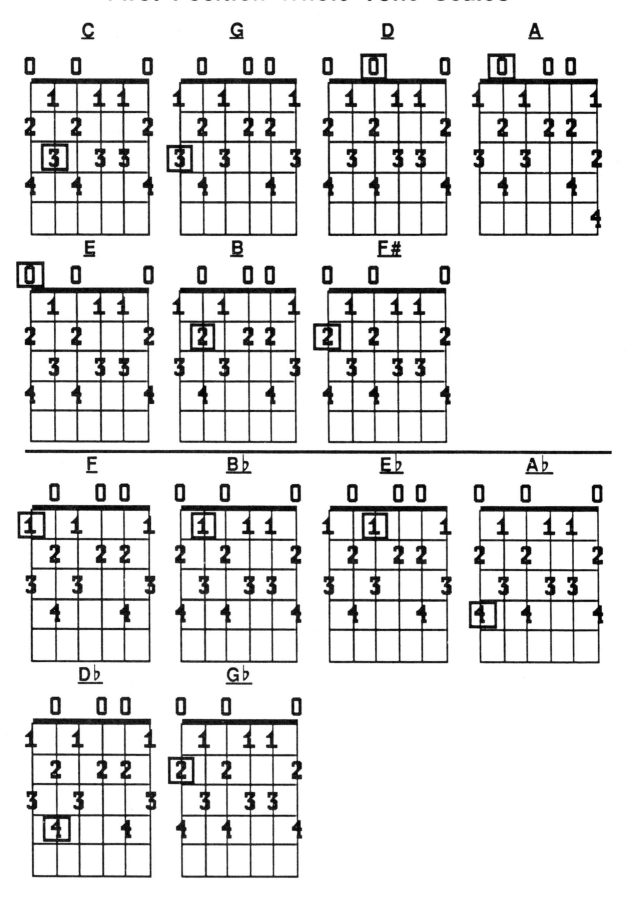

Movable Whole Tone Scales

Type 1

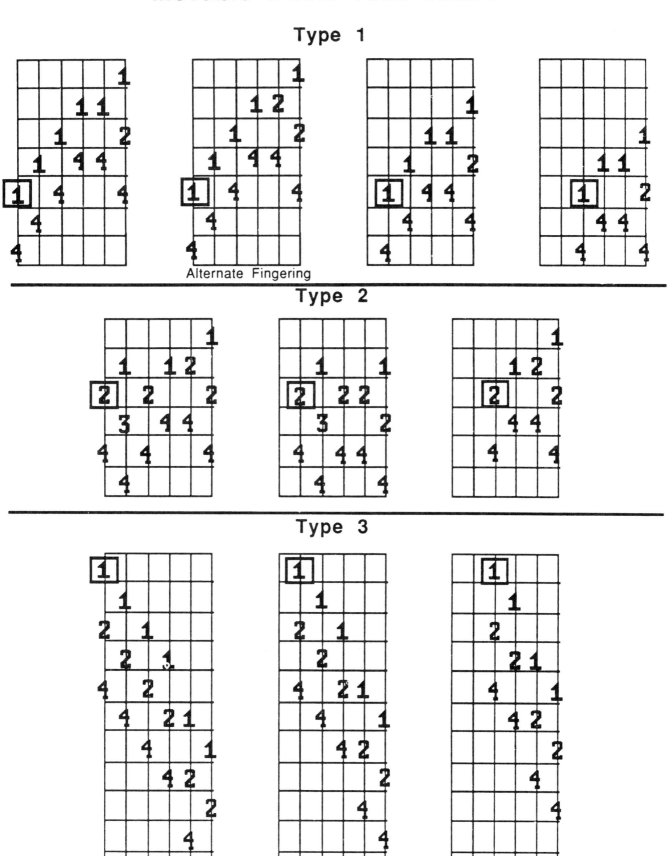

Alternate Fingering

Type 2

Type 3

First Position Augmented Scales

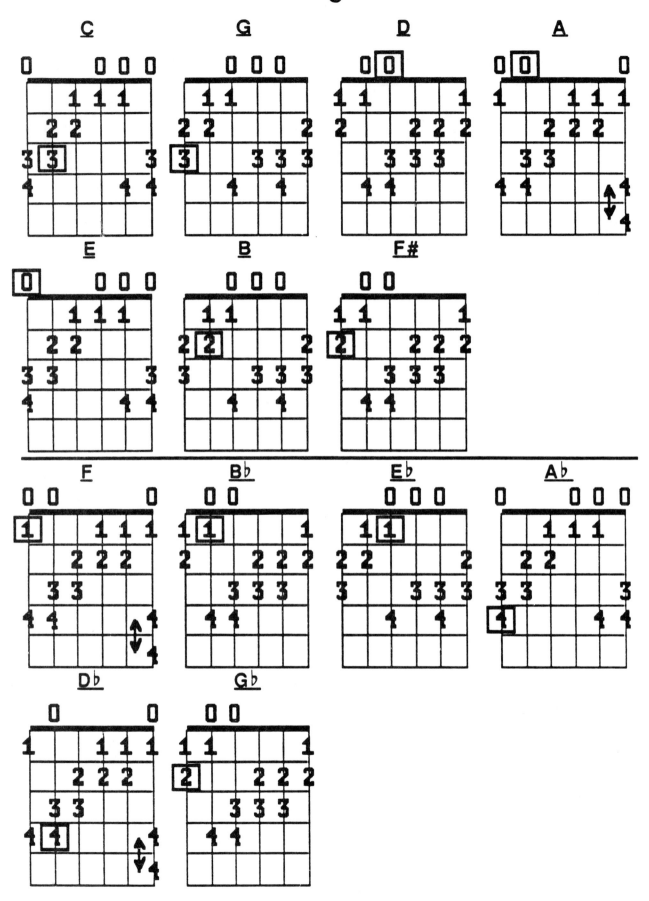

Movable Augmented Scales

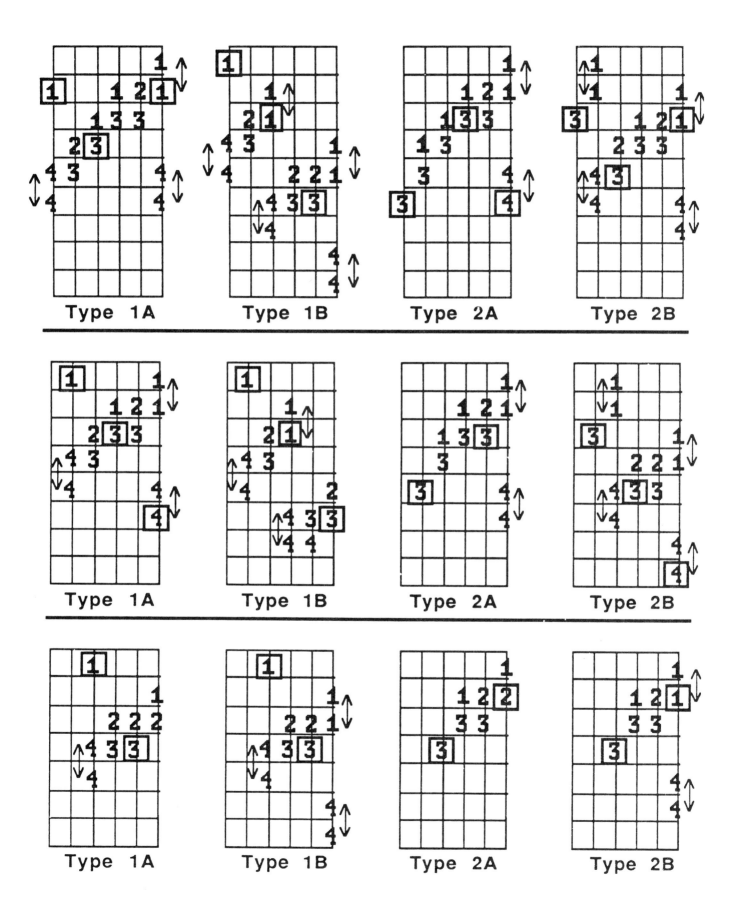

Type 1A   Type 1B   Type 2A   Type 2B

Type 1A   Type 1B   Type 2A   Type 2B

Type 1A   Type 1B   Type 2A   Type 2B

Chromatic Scales

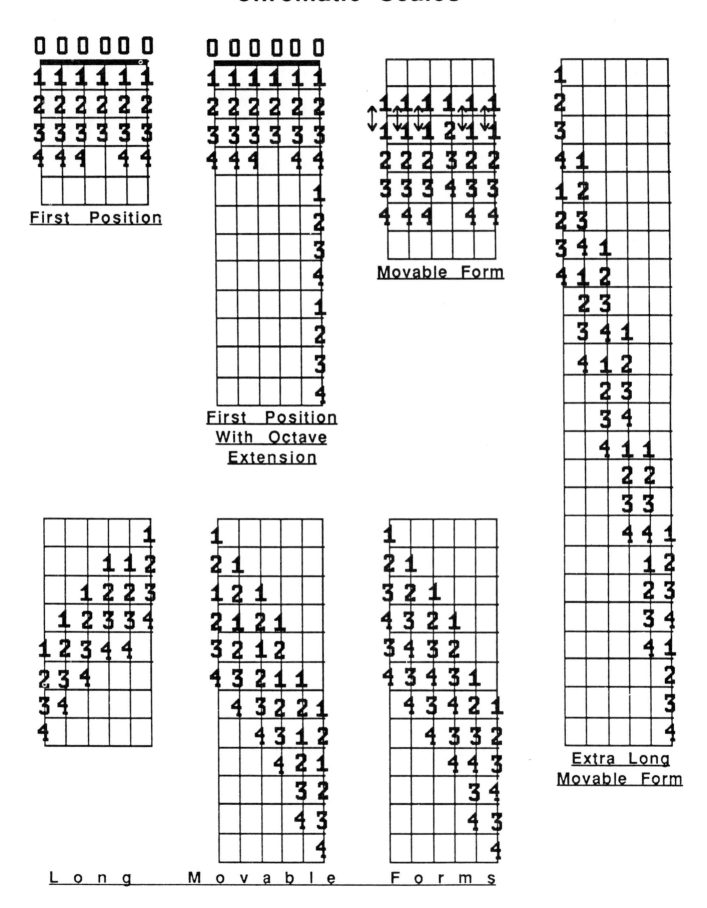

First Position

First Position
With Octave
Extension

Movable Form

Long   Movable   Forms

Extra Long
Movable Form

THE ARPEGGIOS

An arpeggio consists of the notes of a chord played in succession. Arpeggios may be played in any inversion (starting on any note of the chord) and the notes may follow in any order.

Here, all arpeggios are presented in root position (with the root as the lowest note). Wherever the root is repeated in a higher octave it is also boxed. The arpeggios are shown in their convenient, movable, lateral forms the way they are principally used.

The practice of arpeggios helps develop the fingers and the ear (clarifying the sound and structure of chords) and provides basic improvisational materials.

Arpeggios are used simply with their matching chords (CMJ7 chord - use CMJ7 arpeggio). You may also use the following arpeggios as indicated below.

Chord	Arpeggio
Major 9th	Minor 7th from 3rd of chord
Dominant 7th (♭9)	Diminished 7th
Dominant 7th (♯9)	Diminished 7th
Dominant 9th	Minor 6th from 5th of chord
	(or) Minor 7th (♭5) from 3rd of chord

ARPEGGIO INTERVAL FORMULAS

Arpeggios	Intervals				
Major	1	3	5		
Minor	1	♭3	5		
Augmented	1	3	♯5		
Diminished 7th	1	♭3	♭5	♭♭7	
1/2 Diminished 7th (m7♭5)	1	♭3	♭5	♭7	
Dominant 7th	1	3	5	♭7	
Dominant 7th ♭5	1	3	♭5	♭7	
Dominant 7th ♯5	1	3	♯5	♭7	
Major 7th	1	3	5	7	
Minor 7th	1	♭3	5	♭7	
Minor / Major 7th	1	♭3	5	7	
Major 6th	1	3	5	6	
Minor 6th	1	♭3	5	6	
Major 9th	1	3	5	7	9
Dominant 9th	1	3	5	♭7	9
Minor 9th	1	♭3	5	♭7	9

Major Arpeggios

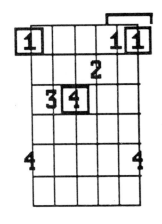 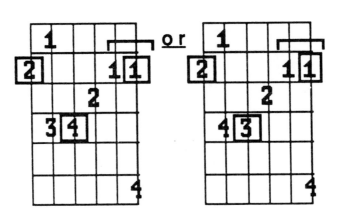 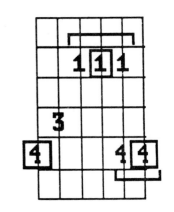

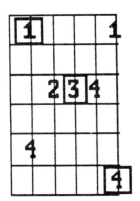 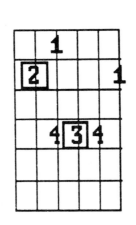 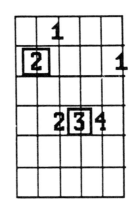 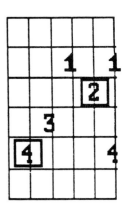

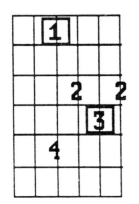 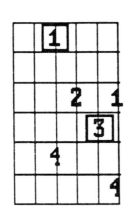 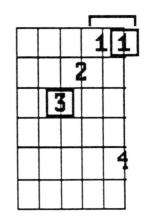 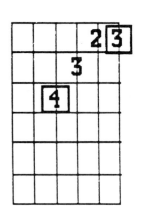

Minor Arpeggios

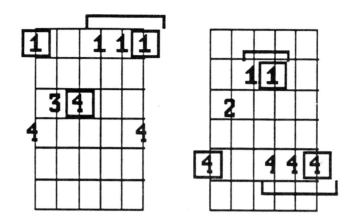

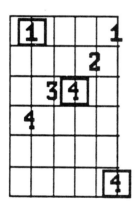 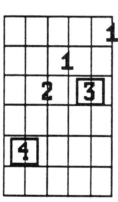 or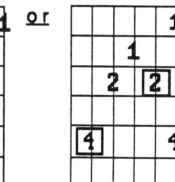

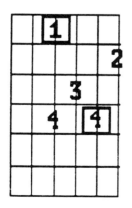 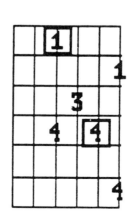 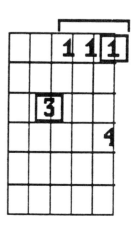

81

Augmented Arpeggios

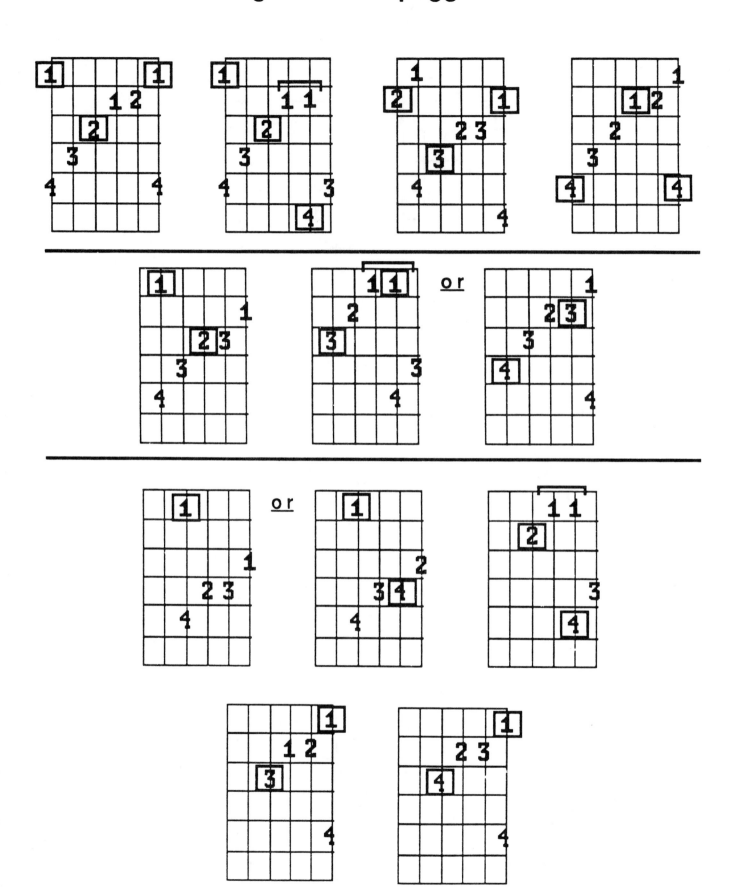

Diminished Seventh Arpeggios

Type 1A

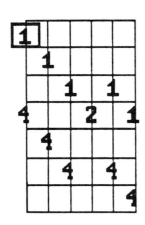
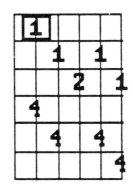
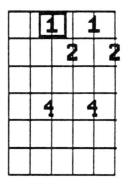
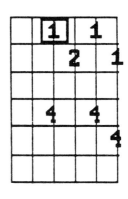

Type 1B

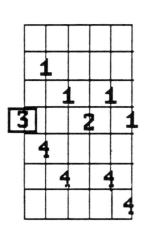
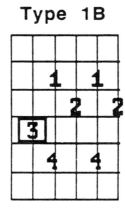
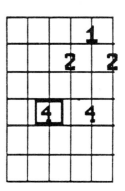
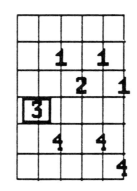
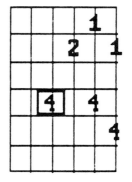

Diminished Seventh Arpeggios
Type 2A

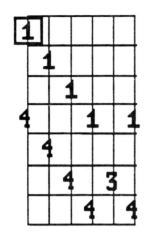

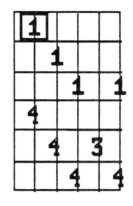

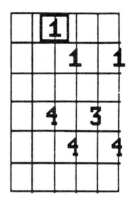

Type 2B

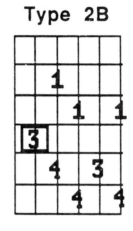

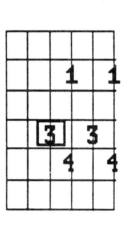

Type 3

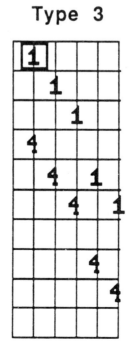

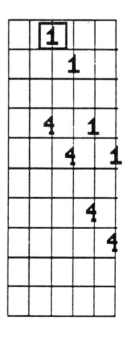

Half Diminished Seventh Arpeggios (m7♭5)

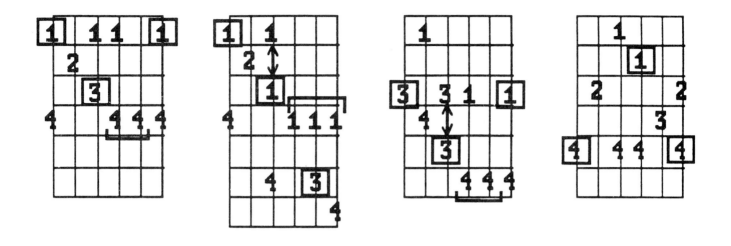

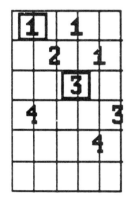 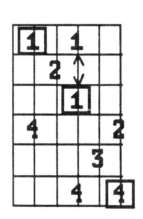 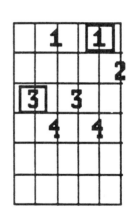 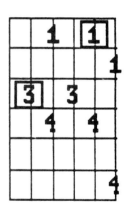

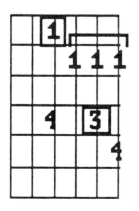 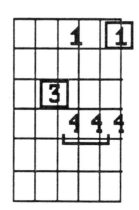 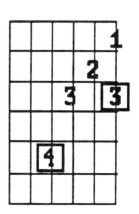

Dominant Seventh Arpeggios

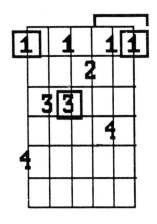 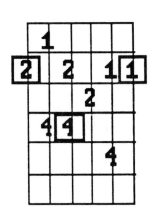 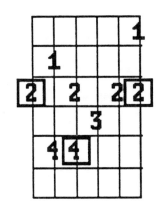 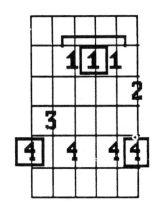

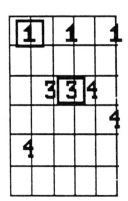 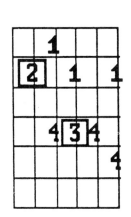 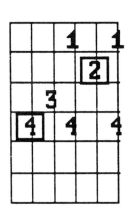 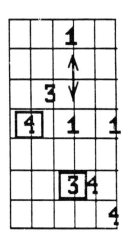

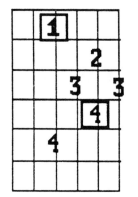 **or**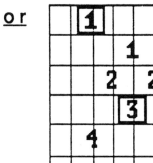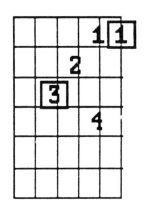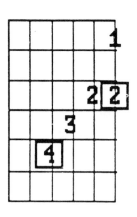

Dominant Seventh ♭5 Arpeggios

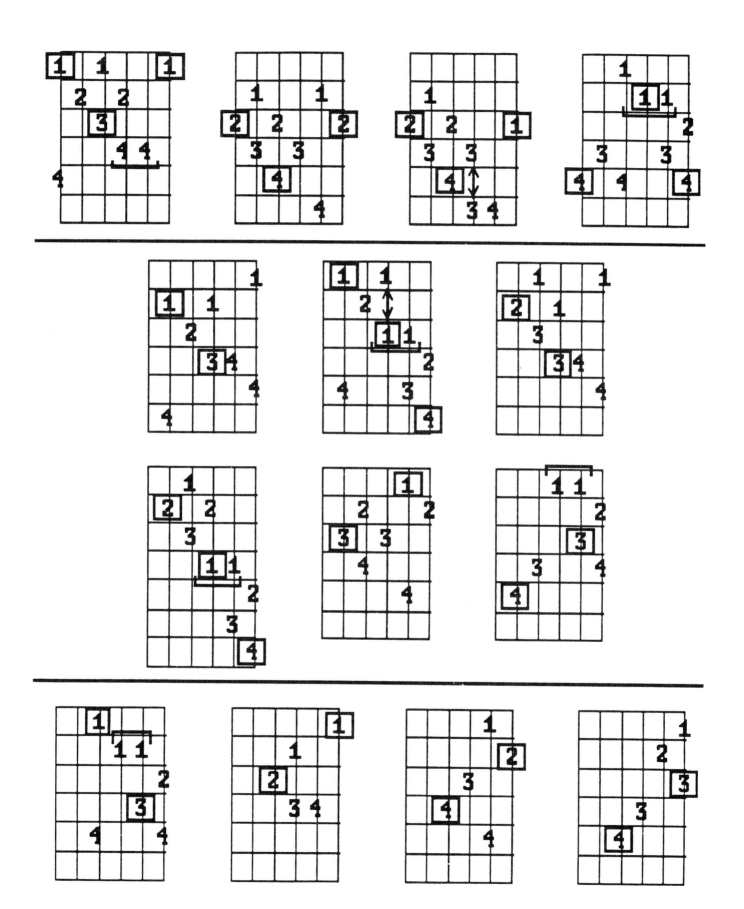

Dominant Seventh ♯5 Arpeggios

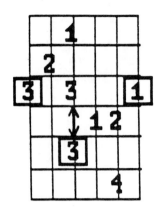
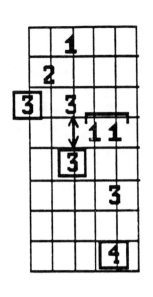
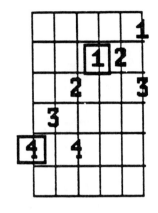
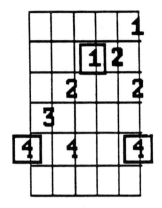

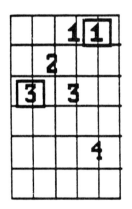
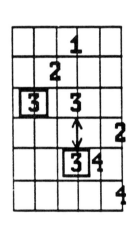
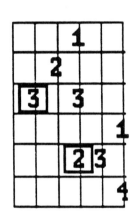
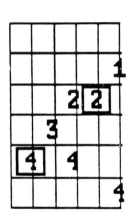

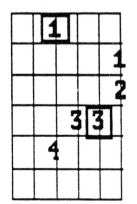
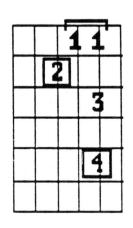
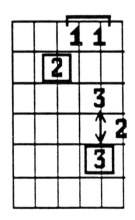
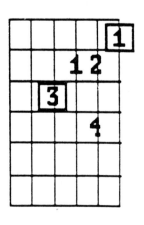

88

Major Seventh Arpeggios

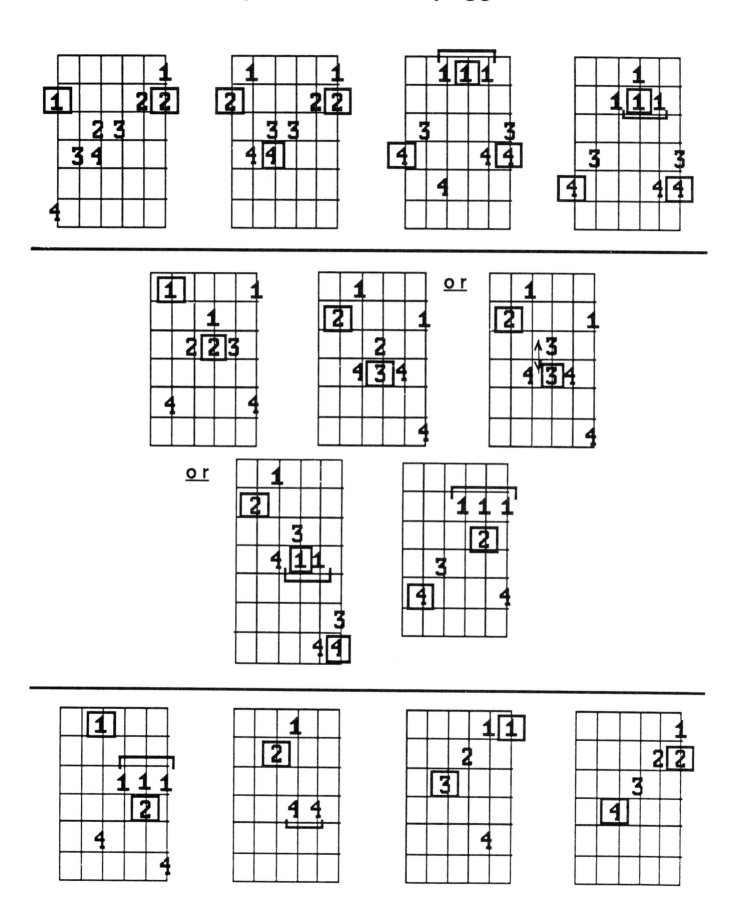

Minor Seventh Arpeggios

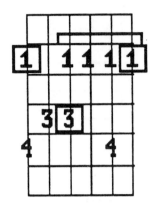
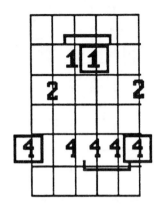

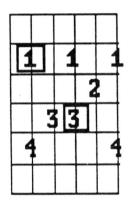
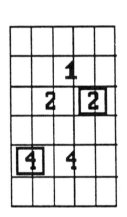
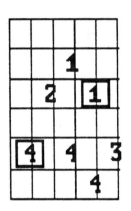
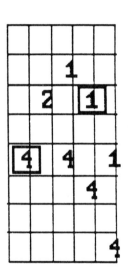

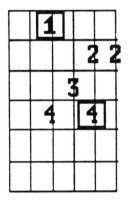
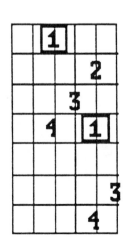
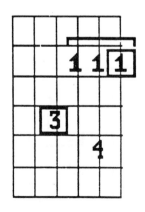
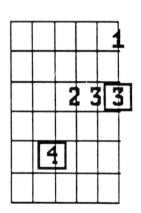

90

Minor/Major Seventh Arpeggios

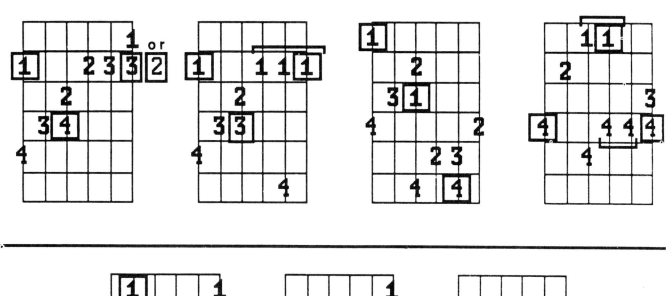

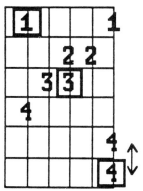 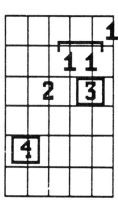 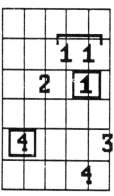

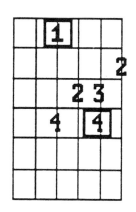 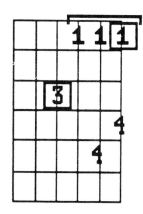 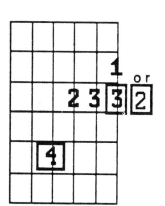

91

Major Sixth Arpeggios

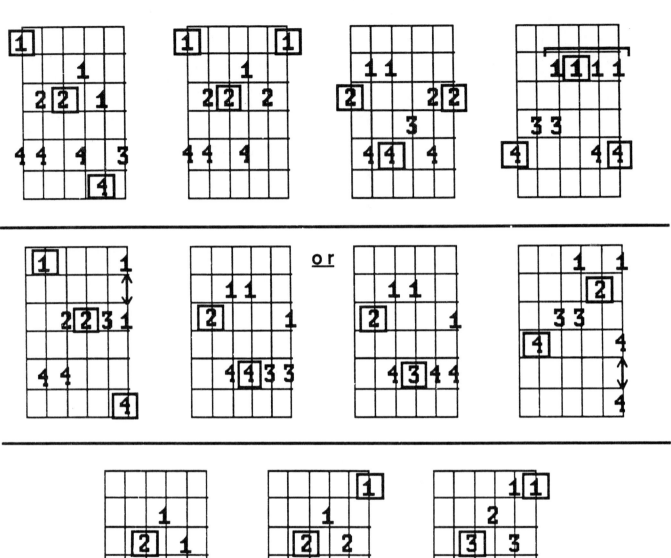

or

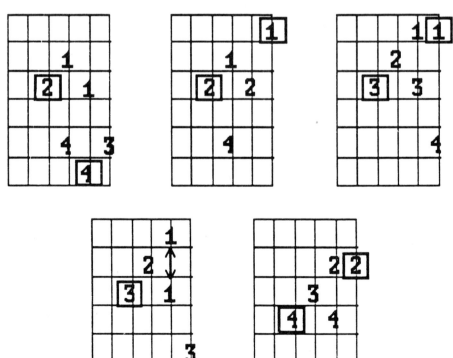

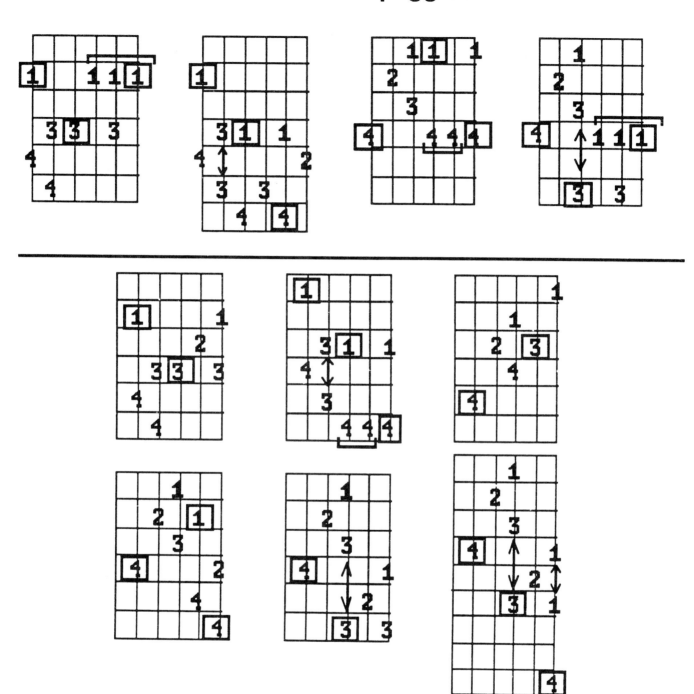

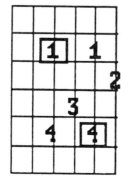
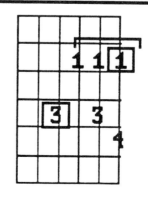

Major Ninth Arpeggios

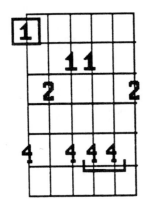
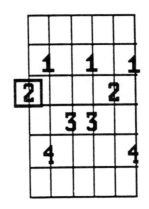
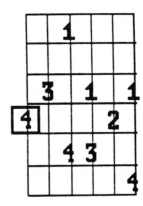

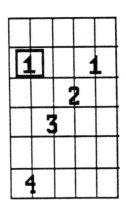
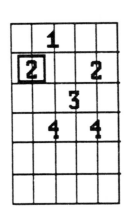
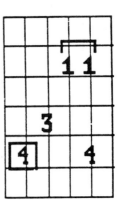

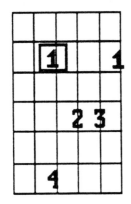
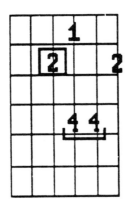
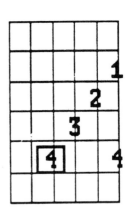

Dominant Ninth Arpeggios

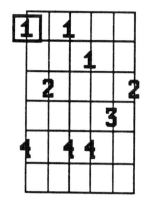 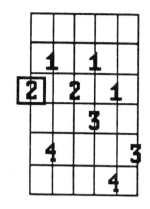 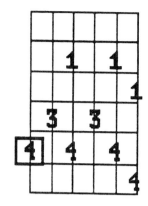

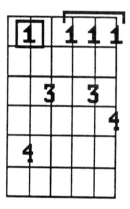 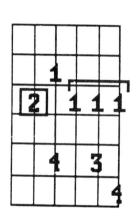 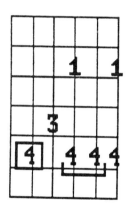

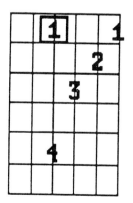 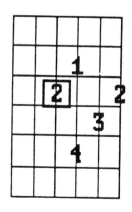 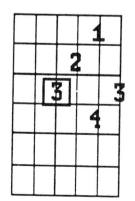 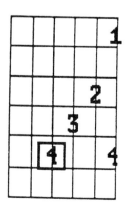

Minor Ninth Arpeggios

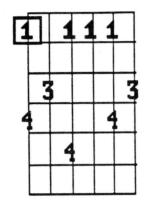

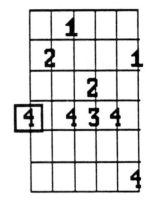

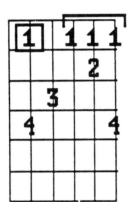

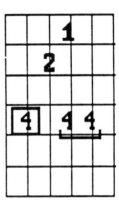

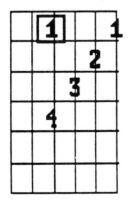

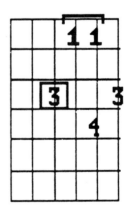